Landmarks of world literature

Constant

ADOLPHE

Landmarks of world literature

General Editor: J. P. Stern

BENJAMIN CONSTANT

Adolphe

DENNIS WOOD

Senior Lecturer in French, University of Birmingham

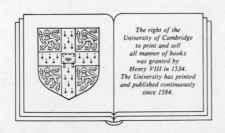

The right of the
University of Cambridge
to print and sell
all manner of books
was granted by
Henry VIII in 1534.
The University has printed
and published continuously
since 1584.

CAMBRIDGE UNIVERSITY PRESS

Cambridge
New York New Rochelle Melbourne Sydney

Published by the Press Syndicate of the University of Cambridge
The Pitt Building, Trumpington Street, Cambridge CB2 1RP
32 East 57th Street, New York, NY 10022, USA
10 Stamford Road, Oakleigh, Melbourne 3166, Australia

First published 1987

Printed in Great Britain at
the University Press, Cambridge

British Library cataloguing in publication data
Wood, Dennis
Constant, Adolphe. – (Landmarks of
world literature).
1. Constant, Benjamin. Adolphe
I. Title   II. Series
843'.6   PQ2211.C24

Library of Congress cataloguing in publication data
Wood, Dennis.
Constant, Adolphe.
(Landmarks of world literature)
Bibliography.
1. Constant, Benjamin, 1767–1830. Adolphe. I. Title.
II. Series.
PQ2211.C24A74   1988   843'.6   87–13101

ISBN 0 521 32822 5 hard covers
ISBN 0 521 31656 1 paperback

GG

Contents

vi   Contents

Preface

No single reading of *Adolphe* can do justice to its immense richness: the present study is no exception to that rule. What I have tried to do in the following pages is to tease out and examine certain strands from the extraordinarily complex web of parallel and contrast, echo and allusion in both characters and situation which is generated and developed in the novel. I hope that I will have encouraged readers to carry on this task for themselves, for it is work essential to an understanding of Constant's art. *Adolphe* is in the nature of a moral conundrum. In order for us to be able to assess the degree of responsibility incumbent on any of its characters, Constant clearly intended that we should proceed by an appreciation of that interplay of character and circumstance which he has arranged with such minute care. I have taken as the starting-point for my analysis the first three chapters of the book: by following the expectations so artfully aroused there through to their frequently paradoxical or ironic realisation, I have sought to emphasise the novel's intricate unity. The chapter I have devoted to the 'portrait' of Ellénore gives, in common with other volumes in this series, an *explication* of a passage of central importance in the novel. Here I have tried to relate linguistic analysis of the kind first demonstrated so incomparably by Erich Auerbach in *Mimesis* to a study of the dramatic situation in *Adolphe*, to the literary tradition in which the novel belongs, and to the framework of social attitudes and assumptions within which it was written.

Limitations of space have necessarily reduced the number of quotations given in French. Nonetheless wherever I have considered it indispensable to provide the reader with the original text I have done so. All translations are my own. For reasons of space, references to the works of other scholars and critics are also brief: further details of articles and studies I mention can be found in the 'Guide to further reading'. Some of the following chapters have benefited from parallel research I am currently undertaking in German and other archives on Constant's early life: I am extremely grateful to the Leverhulme Trust for its support in this work. I should like to thank Professor Alison Fairlie for reading an earlier draft of this book and for making many helpful comments; Dr C. P. Courtney for a number of corrections; and Professor J. P. Stern and Terence Moore, of Cambridge University Press, for their sound advice.

Abbreviations

Adolphe   Benjamin Constant, *Adolphe. Anecdote trouvée dans les papiers d'un inconnu.* Texte établi avec une introduction, une bibliographie, des notices, des notes et les variantes des deux manuscrits et des premières éditions par Paul Delbouille, Paris: Société d'Edition 'Les Belles Lettres', 1977. All references are to this edition.

Cordey   Benjamin Constant, *Cent lettres* choisies et présentées par Pierre Cordey, Lausanne: Bibliothèque romande, 1974.

Fairlie   Alison Fairlie, *Imagination and Language. Collected Essays on Constant, Baudelaire, Nerval and Flaubert* edited by Malcolm Bowie, Cambridge University Press, 1981.

Genèse   Paul Delbouille, *Genèse, structure et destin d' 'Adolphe'*, Paris: Société d'Edition 'Les Belles Lettres', 1971.

Nicolson   Harold Nicolson, *Benjamin Constant*, London: Constable, 1949.

O.C.   Isabelle de Charrière/Belle de Zuylen, *Œuvres complètes*, edited by Jean-Daniel Candaux and others, Amsterdam: G. A. van Oorschot, 1979–84, 10 vols.

Œuvres   Benjamin Constant, *Œuvres*, ed. Alfred Roulin, Paris: Gallimard, 'Bibliothèque de la Pléiade', 1957.

Chronology

(A more detailed chronology can be found in Kurt Kloocke's *Benjamin Constant: une biographie intellectuelle* (Geneva, 1984), pp. 297–374)

	Constant's life and works	*Literary and historical events*
1766		Germaine Necker born, the future Mme de Staël.
1767	25 October: birth of Henri-Benjamin de Constant de Rebecque in Lausanne, Switzerland, the son of Juste de Constant de Rebecque, an officer in the service of Holland. 10 November: death of his mother. Benjamin is brought up by his grandmother.	Voltaire, *L'Ingénu*.
1769		Charlotte von Hardenberg born, Constant's future wife.
1770		D'Holbach, *Système de la nature*.
1772	Juste puts Benjamin in the care of Marianne Magnin, later his father's second wife. Subsequently he is educated in Lausanne, Brussels and Holland by unsatisfactory tutors.	Helvétius, *De l'Homme*.
1774		Goethe, *Werther*
1776		Rousseau, *Rêveries du promeneur solitaire* (1776–8). Gibbon, *Decline and Fall of the Roman Empire*.
1780	Spends two months at Oxford with his father and an English tutor.	

1781		Kant, *Critique of Pure Reason*.
1782	Student at Erlangen University. Fights duels, runs up gambling debts which his father pays.	Laclos, *Les Liaisons dangereuses*. Rousseau, *Confessions*.
1783	Offends Margravine of Anspach-Bayreuth, is recalled by his father. 8 July: arrives in Edinburgh with his father. During the autumn begins studies at the University, joins Speculative Society.	Stendhal born.
1784	Friendship with John Wilde, James Mackintosh and others.	Herder, *Ideen zur Philosophie der Geschichte der Menschheit*.
1785	Leaves Edinburgh (April) without paying gambling debts. Affair with Mme Johannot in Brussels (August). Works on a history of religions.	Mme de Charrière, *Lettres écrites de Lausanne* (first part).
1786	Attempted affair with Mrs Harriet Trevor in Lausanne. Taken to Paris by his father. Frequents the Suard salon, but also gambling dens and brothels.	Germaine Necker marries Baron de Staël.
1787	Friendship with Mme de Charrière. To avoid facing his father in Holland, flees to England, visits friends in Edinburgh (June–September).	Mme de Charrière, *Caliste*, (second part of *Lettres écrites de Lausanne*).
1788	Takes up post as Gentleman of the Chamber (*Kammerjunker*) to the Duke of Brunswick.	
1789	Marries Wilhelmina (Minna) von Cramm, a lady-in-waiting at Brunswick court. Friendship with the writer and freemason Jacob Mauvillon, acquires reputation as a 'démocrate'.	Fall of the Bastille. Declaration of the Rights of Man.
1790		Burke, *Reflections on the Revolution in France*.

1792	Marital difficulties.	Republic declared in France.
1793	Friendship with Charlotte von Marenholz, *née* von Hardenberg. Stays in Switzerland with Mme de Charrière. His republican sympathies become more pronounced.	William Godwin, *Enquiry concerning Political Justice.* Reign of Terror in Paris.
1794	Death of Mauvillon (Jan.). Leaves Brunswick. Meets Mme de Staël in Switzerland (18 September), beginning of their relationship.	Fall of Robespierre. Godwin, *Caleb Williams.*
1795	Arrives in Paris with Mme de Staël. Obtains divorce from Minna von Cramm (18 November).	Directory replaces Convention.
1796	Constant at Coppet with Mme de Staël. He publishes the first of many political pamphlets, seeks French nationality, wishes to make a political career in France.	Bonaparte takes Milan.
1797	He is elected as councillor at Luzarches in France. Begins to weary of Mme de Staël.	*Coup d'état* of 18 Fructidor.
1798	Unhappy with Mme de Staël, wishes to return to a scholarly life. Beginning of his friendship with Julie Talma. Translates Godwin's *Enquiry* (October 1798–January 1799).	Schiller, *Wallenstein* (1798–9). Wordsworth, *Lyrical Ballads.*
1799	24 December: Constant becomes a member of the Tribunate.	Birth of Balzac. F. von Schlegel, *Lucinde.* Bonaparte's November *coup* (18 Brumaire).
1800	5 January: Constant openly hostile to Bonaparte in the Tribunate. November: beginning of Constant's brief but passionate affair with Anna Lindsay. December: renewed unhappiness with Mme de Staël.	Bonaparte victorious at Marengo.
1801	May–July: affair with Anna Lindsay ends in bitter recriminations on her part.	Concordat signed by Bonaparte and the Pope. Chateaubriand, *Atala.*

1802	17 January: Constant excluded from Tribunate because of his opposition to Bonaparte.	Bonaparte consul for life. Mme de Staël, *Delphine*. Chateaubriand, *René*.
1803	Reluctantly follows Mme de Staël into exile in Germany (October).	
1804	Constant meets Goethe, Schiller and Wieland in Weimar. Reads Herder, works again on his study of religions. 29 December: sees Charlotte von Hardenberg (now Mme Du Tertre) for first time in ten years, renews relationship.	Napoleon crowned emperor.
1805	Constant deeply affected by deaths of Julie Talma (5 May) and Mme de Charrière (27 December). Seriously considers marrying Charlotte.	Battles of Trafalgar and Austerlitz.
1806	October: passion for Charlotte, affair in Paris. From this time Constant is torn between her and Mme de Staël with whom he has frequent arguments. 30 October: begins work on a novel out of which *Adolphe* and *Cécile* will develop. 23 November: reads his novel for first time to his friend Claude Hochet. November–December: continues to work on novel. 28 December: reads novel to M. de Boufflers, the reading provokes a violent quarrel with Mme de Staël.	Battle of Jena. Continental blockade.
1807	January: works again on his book on religions. Charlotte seeks a divorce from M. Du Tertre. September: Constant is strongly influenced by the mystical pietistic circle of his cousin Langallerie, an influence that will last some years. 6 December: Charlotte in despair falls gravely ill at Besançon where Constant goes to be at her bedside.	Mme de Staël, *Corinne*.

1808	5 June: Constant secretly marries Charlotte, but is afraid to tell Mme de Staël, whom he joins at Coppet. Completes translation/adaptation of Schiller's play *Wallenstein*.	Walter Scott, *Marmion*.
1809	During the first months of the year Constant probably reshapes his novel to produce more or less the *Adolphe* that we know. His *Wallstein* is published (26 Jan.). 9 May: Charlotte tells Mme de Staël of the marriage. Despite Mme de Staël's efforts to keep it a secret, the marriage becomes public knowledge during the summer.	Goethe, *Elective Affinities*.
1810	Mme de Staël is exiled by Napoleon, copies of her book on Germany, *De l'Allemagne*, are seized and destroyed. Constant works on his study of polytheism and probably on *Cécile*. Dispute over money with his father.	Mme de Staël, *De l'Allemagne*.
1811	Final break with Mme de Staël. Sets up house in Göttingen with Charlotte, writes *Le Cahier rouge*. During the next two years he works in Germany on his study of religions.	Jane Austen, *Sense and Sensibility*.
1812	Death of his father Juste de Constant (12 February).	November: French army in retreat from Moscow.
1814	Constant briefly supports cause of Bernadotte, pretender to French throne. Returns to Paris. Beginning of his hopeless passion for Mme Récamier.	Paris taken by the Allies. Louis XVIII declared King of France.
1815	23 January: gives a reading of *Adolphe* at Mme de Vaudémont's in Paris. 25 March: on Napoleon's return from Elba, Constant rallies to his cause. October: joins Charlotte in Brussels, begins period of semi-exile.	The 'Hundred Days'. Battle of Waterloo (18 June). Napoleon banished to St Helena.

1816	January–July: stays in London, gives readings of *Adolphe* in literary salons. 30 April: hands *Adolphe* to London publisher Henry Colburn. Early June: *Adolphe* appears in London and Paris almost simultaneously (entered at Stationers' Hall, 7 June). 24 June: Constant publishes letter in *Morning Chronicle* denying any link between the novel and his own life. 3 July: his friend Alexander Walker shows Constant his English translation (published September 1816).	Goethe, *Italienische Reise*. Coleridge, *Christabel*.
1817	14 July: death of Mme de Staël. German translation of *Adolphe*.	Stendhal, *Rome, Naples et Florence en 1817*. Byron, *Manfred*.
1818–19	August–February: clandestine correspondence (now in part in Wolfenbüttel archives) and possibly an affair in Paris with an unidentified woman.	
1819	Constant elected Deputy for the Sarthe. During the rest of his life he becomes a leader of the liberal opposition to what becomes, during the 1820s, an increasingly repressive royalist administration.	
1822		Stendhal, *De l'Amour*.
1824	The first volume of his *De la Religion* published. 7 August: third edition of *Adolphe* on sale in Paris.	
1828	Fourth edition of *Adolphe* (Paris, Dauthereau). Constant's health deteriorating.	
1829	June: *Mélanges de littérature et de politique* published.	Balzac, *Les Chouans*.
1830	July Revolution: Charles X deposed, Louis–Philippe becomes King of France. Constant appointed President of	

1831	the Legislative Committee of the Council of State. 8 December: Constant dies. 12 December: state funeral.	Stendhal, *Le Rouge et le Noir.*
1833	Posthumous publication of Constant's *Du Polythéisme romain.*	
1845	Death of Constant's widow, Charlotte.	

Further history of *Adolphe*

1843	Balzac alludes to *Adolphe* in *La Muse du département.*	
1844–6		Sophie Gay, *Ellénore* (novel based on *Adolphe*).
1862–9		J.-J. Coulmann's *Réminiscences* contain a section on Constant.
1867	Published with foreword by Sainte-Beuve.	
1888		J.-H. Menos publishes Constant's letters to his family.
1889	Published with an important preface by the novelist and critic Paul Bourget.	
1889	Published with preface by Anatole France.	
1895		*Journal intime* edited by Dora Melegari.
1907		*Le Cahier rouge* published for first time by Adrien Constant de Rebecque.

1909	Gustave Rudler, *La Jeunesse de Benjamin Constant*.
1919	First scholarly edition by Gustave Rudler, Manchester University Press.
1932	Russian translation prefaced by Maxim Gorki. *Adolphe* illustrates the situation of young men in capitalist societies.
1933	Constant's correspondence with Anna Lindsay and Julie Talma published for first time.
1949	Harold Nicolson's biography.
1951	John Middleton Murry, *The Conquest of Death* (essay on *Adolphe* with English translation).
1977	Critical edition by Paul Delbouille.
1979–84	Correspondence with Mme de Charrière published in its entirety, together with the *Lettres de d'Arsillé fils*, an epistolary novel written by Mme de Charrière and the young Constant.

Cécile published for first time.

Chapter 1

Biographical background

Childhood and education

The author of a novel shot through with multiple skeins of irony and paradox, Benjamin Constant has seemed to many to be himself a tissue of paradoxes. *Adolphe*, a work firmly situated within a tradition of writing that stretches back through the eighteenth century to the age of high French Classicism, to the mid seventeenth century and to the rigorous psychological analyses of La Rochefoucauld, Pascal and *La Princesse de Clèves*, is the supreme achievement of a man who was not himself French but a Swiss Protestant from Lausanne who took French citizenship only in his thirty-first year. In fact his education, both formal and that which he acquired by immense personal labour, was to a large extent English — or more properly Scottish — and German. Henri-Benjamin de Constant de Rebecque was born in Lausanne on 25 October 1767, the son of Juste de Constant de Rebecque, a Swiss aristocrat who was also a military officer in the service of Holland. Herein lies a further paradox: the writer who in literary manuals and histories generally finds himself set alongside Stendhal, Balzac and the other great novelists of nineteenth-century France, in fact lived over half his life in the eighteenth century and his experience of the *Ancien Régime*, Revolution and Directory shaped not only his political opinions but also his literary taste. Constant's mother Henriette died on 10 November 1767, a matter of days after his birth and, although he rarely mentions her, commentators and biographers have seen in his subsequent relationships with women the mark of a man looking for maternal tenderness. (They have also noted his frequent irritation with it once he found it.)

Constant was from his earliest days wholly at the mercy of

a father who was often irascible and capricious, and inclined to be remote, sarcastic and imperious. Yet this father, Juste de Constant, a man given to impulsive and erratic behaviour and, by his son's account, a very poor judge of character (for example, when it came to the choice of a tutor for Benjamin), was also highly intelligent, an honest soldier and a man dedicated to seeing that his only child turned out a well-educated and polished aristocrat and a credit to the gifted if somewhat eccentric Constant clan. The contradictions and inhibitions of Benjamin and Juste are distilled in the portraits of Adolphe and his father, as Constant's close friend Sismondi pointed out when the novel appeared (*Adolphe*, p. 276). Juste loved his son, wanted only what he saw as best for him, was able to express his affection for him in letters, but always found the greatest difficulty in showing emotion when face to face with him. Benjamin for his part, though often puzzled and repelled by his father's blend of authoritarianism and indulgence, returned that affection, made strenuous efforts to please him and in later life flew to his defence whenever he felt him to be threatened. Even as a child Benjamin did not disappoint his father in his high expectations of him: doted on and encouraged by elderly female relatives, he turned out to be astonishingly precocious, expressing himself with great facility and intelligence as the letters which have survived from this period demonstrate. What is also clear is that, although in some respects horribly spoilt, Benjamin was in need of affection. For at the age of four his father had taken the boy away from his grandmother's care and entrusted him to a governess whom he detested, Marianne Magnin, a village girl whom Juste secretly married (Benjamin did not learn that she was his stepmother until many years later). Thereafter Juste unwittingly chose a series of particularly unsuitable tutors for his son, if we are to believe Constant's account of these early years in the autobiographical *Cahier rouge*. Despite his treatment at the hands of these immoral, indolent and even brutal men, Benjamin somehow acquired a very solid foundation of knowledge, which was added to during his year and a half in the care of an English evangelical clergyman who taught him English as well as Greek and Latin.

Benjamin Constant cannot have been an easy pupil: he was headstrong and unpredictable; though extremely quick to learn, he was also very much aware of his outstanding intellect; he shared with his father a capacity for savage and cutting Voltairean irony and found it irresistible to mock those he considered to be blinkered by dogma or decorum. His acute sense of the absurd was often to prove a liability to him in social life. Yet it was also the saving grace in a young man who must have appeared to many to be insufferably vain and condescending. For Constant was seldom able to take himself entirely seriously for long (as the delightful picaresque *Cahier rouge* shows) and his amusement at his own failings and discomfitures was − and remains − contagious. In 1782 he began his university education at Erlangen, in the German principality of Anspach-Bayreuth. Here, despite making some progress academically, Constant succeeded in becoming an embarrassment at the Court of the Margrave by deciding to take a mistress and choosing as the object of his attentions the daughter of a woman who had insulted the all-powerful Dowager Margravine. With that taste for the odd and unexpected in human behaviour which characterises so much of his writing, he records in the *Cahier rouge*:

The strange thing ['le bizarre de la chose'] is that for my part I did not love the girl at all, and as for her she never surrendered herself to me. In all probability I am the only man she ever resisted. But I found consolation in the pleasure of getting people to say that I kept a mistress − and hearing them repeat it to each other − and I was thus compensated both for spending my days with a girl I did not love and for not sleeping with a mistress who was living at my expense. (*Œuvres*, p. 125)

The particular *extravagance* Constant describes here perhaps finds an echo in Adolphe's desire for a 'liaison de femme qui pût flatter mon amour-propre' (Ch. II), 'a love affair which would flatter my self-regard'. Courtiers whom Constant's quick tongue had offended took their revenge on him, now seeing him without an indulgent and powerful protector:

again this is perhaps echoed in Adolphe's conduct in Chapter I of Constant's novel where he acquires a reputation for maliciousness and mockery – perhaps also in the need felt by both Ellénore and Adolphe for a powerful protector who can silence voices critical of them.

Hearing that his son had fallen out of favour at Court, Juste de Constant recalled him from Germany and made alternative plans for his education. He had friends in Scotland, and in view of Edinburgh University's very high reputation at this period, he decided that his son should study there in a suitably serious-minded environment. It proved to be exactly the right choice. Constant spent the 'most enjoyable year' (*Cahier rouge*) of his life there – in fact he was in Edinburgh for some twenty-two months. In the University he followed courses in history and Greek, and at the Speculative Society and other student clubs participated in debates on political, historical and ethical issues. In all probability his lifelong passion for the history of religion, his deep liberal convictions and his skill as a public speaker can be traced to this period. All the evidence suggests that Adolphe's fictional achievement at Göttingen University corresponds closely to the young Constant's actual experience at Edinburgh, where 'by dint of unrelenting hard work' – and very probably while leading 'a very dissipated life' – he did attain a measure of academic success, and that in the medium of English, a language he had only recently acquired.

On his return to the Continent, Constant's first serious love affair – with a married woman, Marie-Charlotte Johannot – was followed by a much stranger (and more characteristic) episode with Mrs Harriet Trevor, a flirtatious Englishwoman who lived in Lausanne. As in the Erlangen fiasco, the parallels with *Adolphe* are striking:

Seeing that most of the young men by whom [Mrs Trevor] was surrounded had designs on her, I decided that I would become her lover. I wrote her a fine letter in which I declared my love, handed it to her one evening and returned the next day to receive her reply. The agitation generated in me by my uncertainty as to the result of this move had given me a kind of fever which somewhat resembled the passion which at first I had only intended to feign.

(*Cahier rouge, Œuvres,* p. 130)

When, on receiving Adolphe's letter, Ellénore tells him that she cannot see him again until the Count returns, Adolphe reacts in a way comparable to that of the young Constant: 'That love which an hour before I had been congratulating myself on accurately simulating I now believed I suddenly felt with great intensity' (Ch. II, p. 124). But Mrs Trevor offered Constant 'friendship', not 'love', and this quibble over a word led to a chaste relationship lasting several months during the course of which her admirer baulked at a verbal obstacle which in all probability was important only to him. At length Constant had to leave for Paris with his father: when he saw Mrs Trevor there three months later, he no longer felt anything for her.

Isabelle de Charrière

During the winter of 1786–7 the young Constant frequented the Suard salon where he met Condorcet and others, and where the talk was of books and politics – in particular of the King's decision to summon an assembly of Notables in an effort to resolve the financial crisis in France. In the midst of this, and while pursuing his other habitual activities – losing money at the Paris gaming tables and making a fool of himself with women – Constant met Isabelle de Charrière, a novelist of considerable talent who had a turn of mind and sense of humour very like his own. There is no evidence that Mme de Charrière and Constant became lovers – she was twenty-seven years older than he – but there can be no doubt as to the great emotional intimacy between them. The portrait of the 'femme âgée' in Chapter I of *Adolphe* seems in large measure based on Mme de Charrière: what is said of this fictional figure and her influence on the narrator –

In my conversations with the woman who had first developed my ideas I had contracted an insurmountable aversion for all commonly held maxims and dogmatic formulae.   (*Adolphe*, p. 114)

– was true in real life of Isabelle de Charrière. Her sharp and probing intelligence undoubtedly developed further Constant's capacity for minute analysis of the anomalies,

adictions and paradoxes in human conduct, so impor-
a feature in the composition of *Adolphe*. Vigilance as
rds language and its power to deceive or dull the mind in
assessment of a situation is a characteristic of many of her
writings as it is of Constant's novel. In the *Cahier rouge* Constant blames Mme de Charrière for bringing out his natural
tendency to a reckless flouting of social convention: in his
novel the elderly woman influences Adolphe in a similar
direction. Nonetheless, during the period of their friendship
Constant appears to have collaborated with her on a short un-
finished epistolary novel, the *Lettres de d'Arsillé fils*, based
on his experiences in 1786–7, the manuscript of which was
published for the first time in 1981 (*O.C.*, IX, pp. 651–78).

Brunswick

In 1788 Constant's father secured for him the post of
Gentleman of the Chamber (*Kammerjunker*) to the Duke of
Brunswick. Though the Duke was a well-read and enlightened
ruler, the seven years Constant spent at his court were probably the darkest of his life: he found its rituals stultifying
and odious, and as time went by his own undisguised enthusiasm for the French Revolution and his republicanism
became equally repellent to those around him. Constant took
revenge on his fellow courtiers through derision, a response
which only isolated him further. Memories of these
Brunswick years undoubtedly found their way into *Adolphe*:
in the ever-present constraints of an all-observing society; in
the sense of futility which oppresses Adolphe in the town of
D*** and makes him look to an affair with Ellénore for some
distraction; in his success in alienating himself from polite
society by his 'plaisanterie perpétuelle', his barbed wit, and
his failure to observe proprieties; above all, perhaps, in an
acute feeling of the sheer power of society that renders individual resistance to it a wearying test of the will. During this
unhappy period of his life Constant's closest friend was the
writer and freemason Jacob Mauvillon, a *démocrate* like
himself and an ardent admirer of Mirabeau (Constant himself

had met Mirabeau in Paris in 1787). Mauvillon was not only an outspoken advocate of freedom of thought and expression and an opponent of censorship, he was also extremely learned in several fields, including philosophy and theology. He undoubtedly had a strong influence on Constant and probably introduced him to German freemasons, whose ideals were not dissimilar to Constant's own.

In 1789, encouraged by the Duke and Duchess and with his father's approval, Constant married a lady at court, Wilhelmina (Minna) von Cramm. The marriage proved a complete disaster. Minna had no sympathy for Constant's intellectual pursuits and soon found his brooding egotism difficult to live with. In 1793, while arranging his separation from Minna, Constant met Charlotte *née* von Hardenberg, the wife of Baron von Marenholz, a man much older than herself. They began a friendship which lasted for several months and which may have been platonic: it appears that Constant was at the same time carrying on a sexual liaison with an actress. Baron von Marenholz generously gave Charlotte not only the freedom to do as she chose, he also gave her an allowance. She was deeply in love with Constant, while he was only mildly involved emotionally. By contrast with the shrewish Minna, Charlotte was gentle and uncomplaining in her relationship with a man who at this period could be very difficult company. Constant soon tired of Charlotte's German Romantic sensibility: as Harold Nicolson puts it, 'he was irritated by the general atmosphere of pink ribbons and *Schwärmerei*' (Nicolson, p. 87), and the friendship was brought to an end by the intervention of Charlotte's father who insisted that she return to her parents and end all communications with Constant. Freedom from a relationship which had grown burdensome coincided with Constant's obtaining a legal separation from Minna. However, relief soon gave way to a characteristic feeling of solitude and desolation at the idea of a final separation of any kind, a feeling which would later be recaptured in *Adolphe*:

They are severed, all my ties, both those which caused my misery and those which were my consolation − all of them! What a strange weakness in me: for more than a year I have longed for this moment, I have yearned for complete independence; now it has come, I shudder with horror! I am utterly crushed by the solitude around me, I am frightened of having no one to cling to, I who complained so bitterly and for so long of belonging to someone.

(Letter to Mme de Charrière, 31 March 1793, *O.C.*, III, p. 593)

Mme de Staël

Constant's bleak years in Brunswick were punctuated by a winter (1793–4) spent in Switzerland with Mme de Charrière, during which the two friends discussed the rapidly changing situation in France. Isabelle was adopting a firm line: appalled by the Reign of Terror and the executions in Paris, she could see little good in the Revolution and was becoming attracted to Counter-Revolutionary ideas. But Constant had lost none of his republican fervour: by the spring of 1794 he went as far as taking up the line of Robespierre, believing that 'the end justifies the means', though this was a position from which he was shortly to retreat.

 He left Brunswick for good in 1794 and on 18 September of that year met Germaine de Staël, an event which profoundly affected his life and career. He was enormously impressed by the intelligence, wit and sheer vitality of Mme de Staël and fell passionately in love with her. At first she did not return that love, and he resorted to threats of suicide: eventually, however, his persistence with her was rewarded. In the summer of 1795 they arrived in Paris together and set about creating a brilliant salon, one dedicated to the moderate republican cause. Both Mme de Staël and Constant were anxious to ward off the possibility of a royalist insurrection or a resurgence of Jacobin fanaticism. In the years that followed they worked both in Paris and at Coppet, Mme de Staël's château on Lake Geneva, to consolidate the good that had come out of the Revolution and to establish a government whose complexion would be essentially bourgeois, rational and moderate. By 1798, however, Constant's relationship with Germaine had become a burden to him: he found her violent passion for him and her possessiveness impossible to bear, yet any suggestion on his part that they end the relationship produced dramatic and emotional scenes which brought them both great suffering. On 15 May 1798 Constant wrote to his aunt Mme de Naussau that Mme de Staël was a tie, a *lien* (as Ellénore would be for Adolphe), but that he felt obliged to stay with Germaine 'out of duty, or if you prefer, out of weakness' until he found a wife (Cordey, p. 77).

On the political front the situation was shortly to take an ominous turn: Bonaparte mounted his *coup d'état* on 9 November 1799. Constant was elected to the Tribunate, a non-voting body which existed to give advice to the First Consul, and he at once dedicated himself to opposing dictatorship and defending individual freedom against the arbitrary exercise of power. He was supported in his courageous campaign by a new (and probably non-sexual) friendship with Julie Talma, a highly intelligent Enlightenment rationalist. Constant's *Lettre sur Julie*, inspired by her death in 1805, at certain points recalls the account of Ellénore's physical decline and death. (In his relationship with Anna Lindsay, Julie was also to play a role akin to that of the 'impartial' woman friend who attempts to reconcile Adolphe and Ellénore, *Adolphe*, Ch. VIII, p. 179.) A daughter of the eighteenth century to the last, even on her death bed Julie Talma refused to see a priest or to receive the last rites.

Anna Lindsay

At the same time as his intellectual friendship with Julie Talma was developing, Constant became involved in the most intensely passionate sexual liaison of his life, with Anna Lindsay. A woman of Irish origin, Anna lived in Paris on the margins of polite society in the manner of the high-class courtesans of earlier times, but the finer aspects of her character had won her society's grudging respect. She was very beautiful and, in Constant's eyes, far more 'feminine' than Germaine de Staël. Some years later Constant wrote of her in his Journal (28 July 1804):

Anna is a woman of distinction. She has great nobility of character and very sound judgement. But she has little subtlety, little variety in her ideas and those opinions [*préjugés*: 'fixed opinions', 'prejudices'] that she has adopted, she has done so from a generous motive and against her own self-interest; there is a fieriness and violence in her and an attention to detail in the way she runs her house which make her a veritable domestic demon. She is perhaps the woman who has loved me the most, and one of those who has made me the most unhappy. But I owe to her all I know of physical and emotional love in women.   (*Œuvres*, p. 344)

The close parallels with the description of Ellénore in Chapter II of *Adolphe* hardly need underlining. Similar words and phrases are used: 'nobility of character', 'sound ideas', 'fixed opinions' (or 'prejudices') that run 'counter to her self-interest', and the 'fire' (*fougue*) and undercurrent of violent feeling in both women. Inevitably Constant's ardour cooled after some months, and, perhaps as inevitably, Anna's grew stronger. As he tried to back away from the relationship gently, as he became more non-committal, so she became resentful, reproachful and jealous. Yet there was about this relationship which continued sporadically for several years a special quality which Constant never forgot. Between him and Anna there was a profound affinity of character: each was full of contradictory qualities and the prey to a deep-seated discontent. Constant commented in his Journal: 'Mme Lindsay writes to me that deep down we resemble each other to an astonishing degree. It is perhaps a reason why we are less well suited for each other . . .' This underlying similarity is in all probability discreetly echoed in *Adolphe*, as is the marginal position that Anna occupied in society. If there was a living model for the Count who keeps Ellénore, the Comte de P***, it would surely be Anna's lover and protector of her and her two children before she met Constant, Auguste de Lamoignon, a French aristocrat whom she followed into exile in Englan d during the Revolution. Lamoignon's condescending attitude towards Anna, perhaps also her 'foreignness' as an Irishwoman in France, and her Catholicism may all have been drawn on in *Adolphe*.

As in the deepening imbroglio of his relationship with Mme

de Staël, Constant was yet again unable to act decisively. He could bring himself neither to continue with Anna in a committed way nor to make a final break. When faced with two options Constant frequently chose both − a feature of his character neatly summed up by Julie Talma who told him: 'vous prenez toujours et ne quittez jamais', 'you are perpetually taking [women] and being unable to leave [them]' (Constant's journal entry for 7 January 1805.) It is obvious that Constant's experience in these two important sexual relationships − and in many others − went into the creation of Ellénore, but in a form so transposed as to rule out any simple Anna/Ellénore or Germaine/Ellénore equation. Whenever Mme de Staël returned to Paris he felt he must be with her: his sense of obligation, his gratitude and affection were analogous to those binding Adolphe to Ellénore. He felt her to be a tyrant towards him, yet he was drawn back to her, thereby provoking Anna Lindsay to paroxysms of jealousy.

Charlotte

Constant's exclusion from the Tribunate in 1802 because of his determined opposition to Bonaparte − whom he viewed as a usurper and a despot − meant the end of any immediate prospect of a political career. The following year he accompanied Germaine de Staël to Germany, met Goethe, Schiller and Wieland in Weimar, and returned to his one consolation in time of emotional distress, his study of religion, work which he continued on his return to France. At the end of 1804 he met Charlotte von Hardenberg for the first time in ten years. She was now remarried to a Frenchman, Alexandre Du Tertre. It was not until 1806 that she and Constant began an affair which, after endless hesitations and *volte-face* on Constant's part, would lead eventually to their marriage. In his journal entry for 26 October 1806 he confessed:

I am tired of the man-woman ['l'homme-femme', a disparaging reference to Germaine's aggressive virile character]. Her iron hand has held me in chains for ten years, and now a truly feminine woman is intoxicating and enchanting me. (*Œuvres*, p. 590)

On 30 October 1806 he began a novel 'which will be our [i.e. Constant's and Charlotte's] story' (*Œuvres*, p. 592) and out of which *Adolphe* and *Cécile* would finally emerge. Constant continued intermittently writing his novel until the end of 1806, then resumed his work on religion. After a relatively calm period spent with Charlotte, he fell once more under the emotional sway of Mme de Staël, with the scenes, recriminations and short-lived reconciliations between them that were by now habitual. During Mme de Staël's absence in Vienna, Constant joined Charlotte, now in great emotional distress, in Besançon: it is at this point that the semi-autobiographical narrative of *Cécile* breaks off, based as it is on this period of his life during which Constant was torn between two demanding mistresses. Over the next three years, despite secretly marrying Charlotte in 1808 and despite her intense suffering, Constant was unable to bring himself to finish once and for all with Germaine de Staël. (It was possibly during 1809 that Constant recast his novel in such a way as to produce more or less the *Adolphe* that we know.) In May 1811 came the final break with Mme de Staël. Constant thereupon settled down to two and a half years of quiet scholarly activity in Germany, living with Charlotte principally in Göttingen and working on his book on religion. (During this period Constant's father died: they had lately been on bad terms because of a disagreement over Benjamin's inheritance from his mother.)

With Napoleon's downfall Constant briefly entertained the hope that the Swedish prince Bernadotte would succeed to the French throne. When this began to appear increasingly unlikely, he returned to Paris to resume his career as a political writer and aspiring politician in the cause of the liberal opposition to Louis XVIII's reactionary government. Constant now made two of the most costly mistakes of his life: his first was to fall hopelessly in love with Juliette Récamier, a well-known beauty who did not return his love and for whom he pined for fifteen months; his second, during Napoleon's brief return to power before Waterloo in 1815, was to draw up an Additional Act to the Constitution for the man whose despotism he had spent many years bravely opposing, and to accept a role as his adviser. Such an about-turn took much explaining and was viewed by many as base opportunism. Constant's explanation was that his aim — the liberty of the individual — had never varied but that he was realistic and flexible about the means to attaining it. Rallying to Napoleon seems to have been the result of a genuine conviction that his aim could be achieved under the ex-Emperor, though it must also be said that Constant was encouraged in his actions by Mme Récamier.

During six months of self-imposed semi-exile spent in England with Charlotte (January — July 1816), Constant allowed feelings in France on his ill-timed collaboration to subside. He gave readings of *Adolphe* at literary salons in London — he may have begun doing so in Germany, and certainly had given readings in Paris — and prepared his manuscript for publication: he was short of funds and there was probably a financial element in his final decision to publish. Constant may have composed the closing 'Letter to the Publisher' and '[Publisher's] Reply' in London in an effort to lessen the likelihood of the reading public making any easy identification between Adolphe and himself or Ellénore and Mme de Staël. If we are to believe the diary of Miss Berry, the literary hostess who attended a reading in February 1816, the novel had not at that point acquired a title (Nicolson, p. 243). After *Adolphe*'s publication in London and Paris in the summer of 1816, Constant returned to the French capital and to an outstandingly successful political career. Elected to the French parliament in 1819, he became known in the last ten years of his life as a brilliant polemicist and defender of liberal causes, and this against a background of increasing royalist reaction. He opposed the slave trade, campaigned for the freedom of the press, became a partisan of Greek independence, and denounced all abuses of political power in France. In 1824 began the publication of his life's work, *De la Religion* ('On Religion'), and in the same year a third edition of *Adolphe* appeared in Paris containing, along with other variants, some paragraphs not found in earlier editions of the novel, those at the end of Chapter VIII which tell of Ellénore's attempts to arouse Adolphe's jealousy: it would seem that they were suppressed in earlier editions because Constant judged them to be in poor taste. They are nevertheless of considerable importance, as they contain a subtly modified 'portrait' of Ellénore which shows her increasing disarray as the plot develops.

During the closing years of his life Constant, who walked on crutches as the result of a fall in 1818, was troubled by ill health and by financial difficulties. He found a source of comfort and consolation in his wife Charlotte. She was at his bedside when he died on 8 December 1830, some months after he had seen the triumph of his liberal ideals in the July Revolution. Constant was given a state funeral that was long remembered. His study of Roman polytheism appeared posthumously in 1833.

Chapter 2

The background of ideas

A new era

Benjamin Constant's character and attitudes in his youth were caught by his Edinburgh friend John Wilde in a character-sketch on which it would be difficult to improve for perceptiveness or concision:

Character of H. B. Constant

By nation a Swiss, by inclination an Englishman, formed to acquire new talents and improve those he already possesses, while, at the same time, he neglects the first, and perverts the second. Feeling the charms of friendship, and yet reasoning against his feelings, a slave to the passion of love, yet varying perpetually in its objects, constant in versatility, in inconsistency consistent. An affectation of singularity forms a conspicuous feature of his character; and this, tho at present attended with disadvantages, may in time prove beneficial, since, if he continue in these sentiments, he must in the end be a Christian. An Atheist professed, he maintains at the same time the cause of Paganism, and while he spurns Jehovah cringes before Jupiter, while he execrates the bigotry and laughs at the follies of superstitious Christians, yet makes the vices of adulterous Deities the subject of his panegyric and prostitutes his genius to support the ridiculous mummeries of its Priests. In politics warm, zealous, keen, invariable, he resembles an Englishman of the purest times; and here, indeed, alone, we find an exception to his general character. He seems, indeed, to have drawn freedom with his first breath, and sucked the principles of liberty with the milk of his Childhood. But it is impossible, in any respect but this, to pursue him thro the endless mazes of his character. He outdoes even Proteus himself. Now he is one thing, now another; your friend, your foe; your advocate, your accuser; he supports you to day, pulls you down to morrow; composes now a panegyric, now writes a satyr; and yet what is strangest of all, to use a simile resembling one in Helvetius, the basis of his character is still the same, for like the sea in a storm, when the surface is agitated by the most dreadfull tempest, and the billows run mountains high, the bottom is still found undisturbed and peaceable.

(See C. P. Courtney, 'Isabelle de Charrière and the "Character of H. B. Constant": a false attribution', in *French Studies*, July 1982)

15

If one leaves aside his very personal enthusiasm for the
religions of Classical antiquity, the young Constant's attitudes were very much those of a French intellectual of the
1780s — a period when the educated classes saw themselves
as uniquely enlightened and reasonable, were growing impa-
tient with Europe's creaking absolute monarchies and longed
to sweep away all that smacked of superstitious prejudice and
of privilege. Constant did not have long to wait before the
ideals he had formed by reading D'Holbach and numerous
other *philosophes* were realised in the fall of the Bastille and
the subsequent dislodgement of the House of Bourbon. During the Revolution and Reign of Terror he was still in his
twenties, young enough to learn and to change — to think
again about his earlier certitudes and to have, in some areas,
new and different ideas. By the beginning of the new century
Constant had the sense of having outgrown an intellectual
and moral world — that of Voltaire, Diderot and the rest —
which he came increasingly to look on as frivolous, self-
seeking and cynical, even though these writers and thinkers
had in some measure prepared the way for a Revolution he
never ceased to defend. Constant's literary style, and indeed
his sense of humour, remained essentially those of late
eighteenth-century France. However his views on a range of
subjects, including religion and politics, were coloured during
the period when he wrote *Adolphe* by consciousness of the
struggle between an old order that was refusing to die — a
world of limited horizons, one based confidently on what he
was to call in the 1824 Preface to *De la Religion* the 'exact
calculations' and 'victorious equations' of enlightened self-
interest — and a new and more generous age. Constant saw
in Germany — which from the 1790s was a formative influence upon him — and in Mme de Staël's circle at Coppet
that some men and women at least were capable of sustained
serious thought and study, realised the hitherto unsuspected
vastness of human ignorance in many areas, had a more
elevated view of morality than the previous generation (here
Kant was a figure of great significance), and were alive to the
importance of the religious dimension in human experience.

In an important book and an article Markus Winkler recently showed that although Constant continued to defend a number of Enlightenment ideals, the world of *Ancien Régime* France and of *philosophes* like the Helvétius whom he had once admired had nevertheless in his eyes been responsible for reducing all relationships and dealings between human beings to the cold arithmetic of personal advantage. As Constant wrote in the Preface to *De la Religion*, the replacement of a disinterested moral code − one which placed value, for example, on self-sacrifice − by one based on expectations of self-interest had had the result of making each individual 'his own centre', his exclusive focus of concern:

Now when each individual is his own centre, all are isolated. When all are isolated, there is only dust. When the storm arrives, the dust becomes a mire.

In the 1800s the climate of ideas was changing, with the tensions and oppositions which we now characterise as the Romantic revolution. But standing in the way of progress towards the kind of world which Constant wanted to see there rose an immovable monolith: Napoleon Bonaparte. Napoleon was for Constant − who remained firmly attached to an Enlightenment belief in human perfectibility − far worse than the traditional hereditary monarch: not only had he halted the natural progress of the French Revolution towards a moderate liberal republic, established an ersatz monarchy and court of his own, suppressed all opposition and embarked on a futile and wasteful programme of world conquest; this military dictator was an 'anachronism' (as Constant calls him in his *Esprit de conquête et de l'usurpation* of 1814). In addition, though two years younger than Constant, Napoleon was a ruler who perpetuated the decadence of an earlier age, the spiritually hollow *Ancien Régime*, of which he was a typical product. As was in the nature of a usurper, the Emperor's contribution to the moral life of his nation had been to promote the unrestricted reign of pleasure-seeking, base cupidity and egoism. Constant was convinced that such hedonism and systematic selfishness − which he saw as the legacy of the eighteenth century — were an inadequate and unworthy response to the complexities of human relationships, especially those between men and women, a response unsuited to his own personality or that of anyone who was remotely sensitive or humane. In all relationships, he believed, the natural demands of sympathy, loyalty, and pity could not be denied. Although in the political sphere Constant tended to view Jean-Jacques Rousseau with suspicion (he held Rousseau's doctrine of the 'General Will' responsible for the Reign of Terror of Robespierre in 1793 and for the tendency of modern tyrants to seek to invade even the inner sanctum of an individual citizen's private thoughts and opinions), there can be little doubt that Rousseau's indictment of eighteenth-century society as sterile, etiolated and artificial struck a deep chord in him, and echoes of it are heard throughout *Adolphe*.

Adolphe, like Benjamin Constant, seems to contain within himself aspects of two different generations, two contrasting climates of thought. It is for this precise reason that, though through a painful process of self-discovery he learns how different his instincts and attitudes are from those prevalent in society — and indeed how much more complex people are than the brittle maxims of his elders will allow, Adolphe nevertheless remains vulnerable to the society which shaped him and by which he can always be tempted. Certainly his relationship with Ellénore reaches an impasse, and he is unhappy at being tied to her: yet what society offers through the Baron de T*** is, as he at length realises, worth far less to him than what he already has.

The Baron himself deserves scrutiny: he is, of course, working in the best interests of his friend, Adolphe's father, in acting as he does, and he would have no hold over Adolphe were not his analysis of the young man's predicament, in part at least, accurate. But one senses that there is something rather more to him and to his role in the story than this, some representative or symbolic value perhaps ultimately related to the author's not uncomplicated attitude to male figures of authority and their power. Surrounded by his court of clever

and amusing men, the Baron seems to epitomise the values —
and the superficial attractions — of an age which Constant
deplored, the Age of Napoleon. Indeed the Baron's will-
ingness to intervene in the lives of Adolphe and Ellénore, his
machiavellianism, his encouragement of Adolphe's *amour-
propre* (Ch. IX, p. 189), his callous attitude towards women
(a trait he appears to share with Adolphe's father, who in Ch.
V takes steps to expel Ellénore from a town in his jurisdic-
tion), and the cruelty of his 'calculations' over the letter
(Ch. X, p. 196) might seem to invite an even more overt
identification — with Napoleon himself, the ultimate
'ministre dont l'âme était usée' (Ch. IX, p. 189), 'government representative who had lost all capacity for feeling'.
(Constant could not fail to remember Napoleon's harsh treatment of one woman in particular — Mme de Staël, whom he
exiled from Paris.). The Baron de T*** is a character whose
cold energy seems to anticipate that of certain figures in
Stendhal's novels, and whose relation to what Michel Delon
has called 'the fatal dynamics of energy' in Romantic
literature would repay further exploration.

Society and the individual

In 1829, some months before the onset of his final illness,
Benjamin Constant published his *Mélanges de littérature et de
politique*. In this collection of writings he saw the idea of
freedom as having been central to all his thought and activity:

For forty years I have defended the same principle, liberty in all
things, in religion, in philosophy, in literature, in industry, in
politics: and by liberty I mean the triumph of the individual — both
over a government that would rule by despotic means and over the
masses who claim the right to enslave a minority to the wishes of the
majority. (*Œuvres*, p. 835)

Constant's was a life across which fell, from beginning to
end, the shadow of *domination* — if not the reality of subser-
vience to another, then the ever-present fear of it. This fear
wrought untold damage in his personal relationships; it
brought out in him qualities of courage and defiance in the

face of political oppression; and it was the source of some of his subtlest insights as a novelist. So frequently viewed as the disciple of Montesquieu because he shared his scepticism and advocacy of religious toleration, Constant was perhaps no less an heir to the radical individualism and libertarianism of Rousseau and of William Godwin (whose *Enquiry concerning Political Justice* of 1793 he translated in 1798–9). It is not surprising, therefore, that running through *Adolphe* is the theme of the intolerable constraints which modern society lays upon individuals, to such an extent that they may be in danger of becoming alienated from themselves. The formation of social attachments, even mere existence with others, may lead to a situation that is restrictive, normative, oppressive: one thinks of Adolphe's father cherishing the expectation that his son will succeed him in his post of government minister, or of what might be termed Ellénore's micro-imperialism. 'So artificial and contrived a society' as that of the princely court of D*** (and no less the other worlds which Adolphe and Ellénore inhabit in Caden and near Warsaw), whose manners and morals are flawed and hypocritical, has an insidious and damaging effect on individual lives.

It is possible to see in *Adolphe* an allegory of the growth and artificial stimulation of *amour-propre* in a young man in whom, as the narrator emphasises, the principal motivation is not self-interest ('I had not, however, the depth of egoism . . .', Ch. I), yet whose first contacts with social life threaten to corrupt his basic good nature. The absence of any link between appearance and reality in the world of polite society – and in the home which is an extension of that society – is likewise stressed: the growing child and adolescent observe with astonishment the gulf between what people say and how they act, between what they appear to be and what they are. In the house of Adolphe's father the outward proprieties are strictly maintained, yet underneath there is a cynically indulgent attitude towards sexual mores. The part-jesting remark that so misleads Adolphe, causing him fatefully to misjudge his own character and enter into a relationship with Ellénore with no serious thought to its continuation, reflects the

attitude prevalent in a corrupting environment. Social com-
petitiveness also plays its part in leading Adolphe to believe
that he must have a love affair. Thereafter Adolphe finds he
is in tragic contradiction with himself. Ellénore, a victim
of society's hypocritical marriage customs and taboos, is
representative of a woman's potential vulnerability in such a
world. She is tormented because her true nature and qualities
go largely unrecognised: only the outward forms matter, and
she has offended gravely against these.

Society, as critics have often remarked, comes to function
almost as a character in *Adolphe*: from beginning to end there
is a sense of its power and corrosive effect on the individual.
Adolphe has a *cœur naturel* (Ch. I, p. 115), a natural heart:
spontaneously he reacts against society's artificiality and
hypocrisy, but at length he is brought under its sway. He
becomes guilty of duplicity – a thing remote, we are told,
from his 'natural character' (Ch. IX, p. 190) – because of the
impossibility of his position with Ellénore, of course, but very
specifically as a result of the intervention of the Baron de
T***: he lets the Baron believe he will leave Ellénore, while
he hides from Ellénore the Baron's intention of separating
them. In the narrator's comment, 'l'homme se déprave dès
qu'il a dans le cœur une seule pensée qu'il est constamment
forcé de dissimuler' (Ch. IX, p. 190), 'man becomes cor-
rupted from the moment there is in his heart a single thought
he is constantly obliged to hide', there is, perhaps, a political
undertone: Adolphe is brought to a position where he is not
free to express his feelings in their full complexity to anyone,
and his behaviour alters for the worse. It is surely not without
significance that *Adolphe* was written when France had effectively become a police state under Napoleon's minister
Fouché and was controlled through an elaborate network of
spies and informers.

If there is a more general political and moral parable to be
found in *Adolphe*, it would seem to centre on the unhappiness
created by a heartless society that promotes values based on
'the exact, impassive, invariable calculations of enlightened
self-interest' (*De la Religion*), a society which is intolerant of

individual citizens who resist such an ideology, and which enforces impossible choices between the public and private spheres. Though *Adolphe* appears to portray the Germany Constant knew in the years 1788–94, in all probability he had in mind conditions in the society of Napoleon's France during the years 1806–9, the period when the novel reached the form in which it is read today. Adolphe, 'in many ways a prototype of the liberal individual' according to Stephen Holmes, would seem to represent the lot of modern man in such a society: he is oppressed throughout the story – by the authority of his father, by the tyranny of Ellénore (her *empire*, her *despotisme*), by *l'opinion* – what society thinks. In finally achieving what society wants of him, the abandonment of Ellénore – a demand he desperately repudiates, but too late – Adolphe becomes permanently alienated from that society and from himself.

Chapter 3

Adolphe: the narrative and its framework

Readers opening *Adolphe* for the first time are impressed by the lucidity and elegance of the narrative and by the steady, almost hypnotic intensity of the narrating voice, that of the older Adolphe: they are drawn to respond to the intelligence and depth of his insights on his past experiences, the extraordinary complexity of his feelings as described in the central chapters and the overwhelming sense of tragedy in the final pages. For anyone familiar with the facts of Constant's life, the events of the novel seem to mirror forty years of dilemmas and inconsistencies in his relationships with his father and with a series of women, years which were to culminate in his marriage to Charlotte von Hardenberg. (One might add parenthetically that this last relationship, not always an untroubled one, may have been in Constant's mind along with the others when he wrote *Adolphe*: Charlotte's mother's name was Eléonore; the pet names which Constant and Charlotte had for each other – 'Ouffy' and 'Linon' – sound oddly close to Adolphe and Ellénore; and Charlotte's sheer 'ordinariness' of mind was a frequent source of irritation to him.) The novel's intimate connection with Constant the man has never been in doubt. However, such parallels and the fact of *Adolphe*'s first-person narrative have led all too often to its being read as a personal confession, which it is not. Though *Adolphe* may echo many of Constant's experiences and emotions, it is nevertheless an artistic invention, a work of fiction, and the voice of its narrator is not Constant's.

While rejecting this tendency to see *Adolphe* as a *roman à clef*, a mere jigsaw puzzle of biographical data, modern critics have sometimes been inclined to see in it a different type of mystery – the potential presence of an 'unreliable narrator' of the kind found in a number of twentieth-century novels, where it is the novelist's deliberate intention to signal to readers — as it were over the narrator's shoulder — that what is being said is not to be taken at face value. Searching for some cryptic mechanism and message is liable to lead to a distorted conception of *Adolphe*, and to make us overlook the nature of the novel's genuine originality. We may be irritated or even enraged by Adolphe's account of his behaviour, we may judge him severely on the evidence he provides about his relationship with Ellénore, but Constant has not built into Adolphe's narrative some concealed system of indicators which, once found, would enable the reader to 'catch Adolphe out' — catch him, that is, in the act of dissembling and deceiving, of trying to hide from us the full truth about his past conduct and motivation.

There is a distance, an inevitable one, between the young Adolphe and the man who recounts how that young man's hopes and ambitions effectively came to an end: it is the gulf between ignorance and an understanding for which the narrator has paid a very high price. From the opening pages that gulf is repeatedly marked out — 'at the time I did not know what shyness was', 'this [concern with death] has receded as I have grown older', and so on. Though changed by his experiences, the narrator remains essentially the same person, — 'a lack of spontaneity which even today my friends reproach me for'. Constant uses the conflicting perspectives of the narrator who puts pen to paper and of the young Adolphe, whose attitudes coincide with the events related in the story, in order to create a certain mood. The narrator's tone is rueful and prophetic, and the reader senses that his story will end unhappily. But there is more than this: as the story progresses the older Adolphe's attitude to what he is recounting undergoes a significant change. From the cool and self-assured note of the opening pages — 'Je ne veux point ici me justifier: j'ai renoncé depuis longtemps à cet usage frivole et facile d'un esprit sans expérience' (Ch. I, p. 115), 'I in no way wish to justify what I have done: I long ago gave up such a frivolous and facile practice typical of an inexperienced mind' — the narrator is brought to expressions of regret — 'Certes, je ne veux point m'excuser, je me condamne plus sévèrement qu'un autre peut-être ne le ferait à ma place' (Ch. VIII, p. 186), 'Certainly I have no wish to excuse what I have done: I condemn myself more severely than perhaps another man might do in my situation.' As he recalls and relives his past, the narrator's air of detachment diminishes noticeably: he becomes increasingly agitated and his style more exclamatory, as in the case of his last sentence in Chapter VIII and the aside in Chapter IX, 'La pauvre Ellénore, je l'écris dans ce moment avec un sentiment de remords, éprouva quelque joie de ce que je paraissais plus tranquille' (p. 189), 'Poor Ellénore — I write this now with a feeling of remorse — was happy that I seemed more settled.' Timothy Unwin has pointed out in a perceptive article that the narrative is an emotional crescendo which reaches its climax with Ellénore's letter of reproach: thereafter the narrator is silent, as indeed he most often is when observed by the 'Publisher' in Italy.

It is a far cry from this to argue that Constant sets out deliberately to undermine the credibility of the narrator from within: that is, to display *through Adolphe's very narrative* a man who is visibly devious and a dissembler. Constant does not create an 'unreliable narrator' in the modern vein. His strategy is different and offers still more possibilities for widening our judgement of what happens in the story. He places around the narrative a number of 'framing' passages which expand our knowledge of Adolphe's later life and pass judgement on his conduct. Outside the novel of which these passages are still a part there are Constant's own two Prefaces, for which there are manuscript variants. While some degree of caution is obviously necessary when handling these Prefaces — the second of which at least was composed many years after Constant's first impulse to write the novel (D. H. Lawrence's advice 'Never trust the artist. Trust the tale' is perhaps salutary in this connection) — the *Avis de l'Editeur*, 'Publisher's Note', *Lettre à l'Editeur*, 'Letter to the Publisher', and *Réponse*, 'Publisher's Reply' are of considerable importance to our understanding of *Adolphe*.

The 'Publisher's Note' which precedes the narrative shows Constant re-using a somewhat threadbare device familiar from many eighteenth-century novels, most notably Marivaux's *La Vie de Marianne* — the pretence that a manuscript was found by accident — and putting it to a new end. Although, as the *real* manuscript of this section shows, he may have begun with the idea of the (imaginary) manuscript lying alongside a hoard of diamonds, the final version shows Constant using the 'Note' to give us a portrait of Adolphe as he is after the loss of Ellénore, with three sentences from him which reveal his despair and bitterness: the ironic comment to the village surgeon introduces us to Adolphe's characteristic mode of thought. He is presented in a deliberately un-Romantic way: Chateaubriand's René had been portrayed amongst the ruins of Rome, but Adolphe is not interested in anything or anyone; he is always alone and racked by some unexplained inner torment. The notation is spare: by day he sits with his head in his hands, in the evening he walks by himself. His pain is real and intense, not an occasion for striking poses. This image of suffering remains in the reader's mind during everything that follows.

However, the Note's real originality lies in its being linked firmly to the Letter to the Publisher and Reply through the fact of the Publisher's meeting a man in Germany who had known Adolphe and Ellénore and who has in his possession letters which throw light on Adolphe's fate after Ellénore's death. The Letter and Reply offer differing views of the man each writer has known in the light of the 'anecdote' found in the notebook mentioned in the Publisher's Note. They are views which recapitulate at certain points precise moments in the story (the 'mixture of egoism and sensibility' in the Letter, for example, takes us back to Ch. I), and offer different assessments of what is responsible for the tragedy which it relates. In doing so they offer a challenge to the reader's response to the narrative, and an encouragement to us to clarify our thoughts on it. As Alison Fairlie has pointed out, the technique had been used by Chateaubriand at the end of *René*, where the sympathetic Chactas and the severe Father

Souël each comment on what they have heard, but in *Adolphe* the device reaches a new degree of sophistication. The writer of the Letter to the Publisher has read Adolphe's story and returns the manuscript, saying how many sad memories it has revived. His attitude is essentially one of sympathetic understanding for both Adolphe and Ellénore: for him Adolphe is a 'strange and unhappy' man and a man who has done wrong, while Ellénore is 'worthy of a kinder fate'. Yet what is so interesting and finally stimulating about the Letter and the Reply to it are the number of questions that are left unanswered, the number of points that are *missed*. In the Letter Ellénore's shrewishness is completely elided, that whole 'tyrannical slave' side of her which so exasperates Adolphe. She is seen as 'worthy of [being loved by] a more faithful heart': yet it can be argued that Adolphe, despite ceasing to feel passionate desire for her, makes enormous sacrifices for Ellénore and — with the exception of his fatal moment of weakness with the Baron — *is* by and large loyal and faithful. And does he, as we are told in the Letter, 'keep her by a kind of spell under his domination'? The question of who dominates whom in the story is in fact far from clear, as every reader knows. The writer of the Letter had tried, he says, to arm Ellénore's 'reason against her heart', believed he had succeeded in bringing about her separation from Adolphe, and then, returning after a long absence, found she had died. The Letter-writer's efforts are surely meant to put us once again in mind of that key scene in Chapter VI where Adolphe genuinely tries to tell her that they must see reason: the consequence is Ellénore's hysteria and fainting-turn and Adolphe's reluctant deceiving of her. Like Adolphe on that crucial occasion the Letter-writer had also failed, hence perhaps his degree of sympathy for Adolphe, whom he sees as a complex, tormented man finally deserving of pity. The writer of the Letter echoes Adolphe's words in Chapter VI when he says that Ellénore's unhappiness proves that 'even the most passionate feelings cannot struggle against the order of things', that 'society is too strong': Adolphe had told Ellénore 'one struggles for a while against one's destiny and finishes by surrendering. The laws of society are stronger than men's wills; even the most powerful feelings are destroyed by the fateful nature of circumstances' (p. 163). This verbal thread leads us back to a central moment in the novel: it is an invitation to the perceptive reader to become a critic. When the Letter to the Publisher describes society's power as reproducing itself through many agents, we remember the narrator's reflections (Chapter VIII, second paragraph) on dispassionate third parties who believe that they understand what is knowable only from within a relationship. These reflections anticipate the 'oeil indifférent' (Ch. X, p. 196), the coldly 'objective viewpoint' of the Baron de T*** who, although he is now beyond passionate feeling, vaguely recollects in Chapter IX that in his youth love affairs had brought him pain. Yet if it is he, a man 'incapable of affection', that the Letter-writer has in mind here, it is not the sight of Adolphe's affection for Ellénore that makes him 'attack and destroy it', but concern for Adolphe's father and for Adolphe's long-term future that leads him to act as he does. Again the point is *missed*: in his urge to criticise society, the writer of the Letter neglects the nuances — which is precisely the only place where the complex truth can be found. His summing-up thus again shades off irritatingly — and provocatively — into inaccuracy, spurring the reader to be a better judge. Even as he writes to the Publisher about unhelpful third parties who interfere, he himself demonstrates how easy it is to miss the vital truth about an experience one is not involved in (a theme reiterated throughout the story) — and how easy it is for the reader and critic, once the book has been put down, to imagine a story other than the one that has just been read. It is a most unusual and daring exercise to build into a novel at this period such a suggestive and cautionary parallel: the outsider who cannot know how it feels to be inside a unique relationship, and the reader who is obliged to attend very carefully indeed to every small detail of the story or risk misunderstanding and misjudgement.

The Letter is linked to the Reply by the Letter-writer's belief that the 'anecdote' will be 'useful' and 'instructive'. To this the 'Publisher' rejoins with withering scepticism, to the effect that one derives instruction only from one's own personal experience, and that readers will fail to see a closeness between themselves and the characters in the story. The didactic view of art expressed in the Letter is thus opposed, and one calls to mind Constant's well-known remarks on the moral purpose of art in an essay on Mme de Staël and her work, dating from 1829 (though perhaps based on an earlier manuscript) but reflecting his lifelong opinion: 'A work of imagination must not have a moral purpose but a moral result. In this it must resemble human life, which has no purpose but always has a result in which morality necessarily has its place' (*Œuvres*, p. 868). In an age of often gross didacticism, exemplified notably by the novels of Mme de Genlis, Constant always maintained Kant's distinction, that art is 'zweckmässig', purposive, but has no 'Zweck', no precise goal or purpose: art has purposiveness without having a purpose, its nature is to raise problems but not to solve them. The Publisher agrees to publish Adolphe's manuscript since it is 'a truthful story of the wretchedness of the human heart' (interestingly Miss Berry who heard Constant read *Adolphe* in London before its publication calls it 'a sad and much too true story of the human heart' − perhaps it was so described by Constant himself before this phrase found its way into the Reply, which may have been composed later in 1816). The phrase has religious − indeed Pascalian − undertones which are maintained throughout the Reply (the 'misère' of the human heart is a central theme of Pascal's *Pensées*). Taking the side of Ellénore completely, the Publisher sees the story as demonstrating: that the intellect cannot bring happiness (certainly a defensible interpretation, but what if one is born an intellectual?); that strength of character, firmness, fidelity and kindness are gifts for which we must pray to heaven (but again, must one wait on a miracle if one does not possess them, the reader may rightly ask); the Publisher, seeming to refer to the same key scene in Chapter VI as the Letter-writer, does not consider Adolphe's moment of pity as a true mark of kindness. In a relentless rhetorical crescendo he characterises Adolphe's arguments as ingenious sophistry which can never justify what he has done. Balanced phrases set explanation, description and self-analysis against the making of excuses, pity-seeking and feeling genuinely sorry, the last being the only appropriate response the circumstances demand of Adolphe in the Publisher's eyes. Alison Fairlie is surely right to raise the parallel with Chateaubriand's Père Souël: the Publisher takes the moral — in fact apparently the severe Christian view — of Adolphe's conduct, and thereby widens further the range of responses to which the reader is exposed. Yet, impressive as the Publisher's Reply is, building antithesis upon antithesis, general statement on general statement in swelling diapasons, driving home through repetition ('I detest') abhorrence for Adolphe's behaviour — and this is undoubtedly one of the most memorable passages in the whole of French literature — we must nevertheless be on our guard. For are we not put vividly in mind of the 'well-established principles' (Chapter I) of those whom it pleases to lump together morality, social forms and religious belief, and whom Adolphe was drawn to contradict with his instinctive wariness of 'those general axioms so free of exceptions and nuances'? Are we not brought full circle and reminded of the kind of thing which Adolphe had stood out against? After the Letter to the Publisher with its sympathy for Adolphe, its critique of society and its mixture of accurate and highly debatable statements, we now have the seductive rhetoric of condemnation, which can also err. The famous and compelling sentence about 'the pain one causes others' is surely, on reflection, rather beside the point, since no one is more anxious to spare Ellénore suffering than Adolphe, and the reasons for his ultimate failure to do so are too intimidatingly complex and interconnected to justify simple condemnation. And again, Adolphe could hardly be described as 'soaring indestructible above the ruins' he has caused: such a view in fact conflicts with what the Publisher has himself seen in Italy. It also takes some stretching of the imagination to see all the evil in the story as imputable to Adolphe's weakness alone and not, in part at least, to those around him or to the social order in which he must live, whether in Germany, Bohemia or Poland. Certain flaws of character may punish him for defects elsewhere in his make-up, but − even if one's experience of reading the novel closely did not contradict it − it would be hard to imagine the novelist who could see the power of 'the social order [and] the action of society on the individual' as equivalent to the gods of Greek tragedy (*Œuvres*, p. 952) as underwriting the statement by the Publisher that 'circumstances count for little, character is everything'.

The last word on Adolphe − and a magnificent word at that − is thus given, with appropriate irony, to a defender of the social group of whose over-simplifications and easy categorisations Adolphe had been so critical. The Publisher's judgements send us mentally back to Chapter I. Thus the novel becomes in its final pages a formidable hermeneutic puzzle, generating its own − deliberately *dissatisfying* and contradictory − self-critique: it is a masterly lesson in reading and mis-reading, perhaps without parallel among nineteenth-century novels, which, even without Constant's Prefaces, not only leaves *Adolphe* open-ended and problematic on every issue, but remains a permanent incitement to re-explore the book.

Chapter 4

Adolphe: the art of paradox

Structure

The plot of *Adolphe* appears to be quite deliberately marked out with a number of caesurae which signpost an unmistakably decisive shift in the action, the close of one phase of activity and the beginning of another. These occur three times and coincide with the endings of chapters. (Though Constant's chapter-endings are seldom weak, three of them especially give the reader the sense of the curtain closing on an act or 'movement' that is now irrevocably completed.) At the close of Chapter III Adolphe, in a state of euphoria, thanks Nature for the enormous blessing she has bestowed on him in giving him physical possession of Ellénore: Adolphe's remembered exhilaration is emphasised by repetition, 'pour la remercier du bienfait inespéré, du bienfait immense qu'elle avait daigné m'accorder', 'to thank her for the unhoped-for favour, the immense favour she had deigned to grant me'. (The following chapter, after a passage of reflection on happy lovers, 'Charme de l'amour', brings us swiftly to Adolphe's growing disillusionment.) The second phase of the story closes with the end of Chapter VI: Adolphe and Ellénore are travelling to Poland and memories of their shared experiences rekindle tender feelings in Adolphe, but although he occasionally speaks to Ellénore as though he still loves her, his emotions are likened, in a memorable image, to a few last pale leaves put out by an uprooted tree. The third 'movement' of the novel ends with Chapter IX, where the narrator speaks of the fateful letter to the Baron de T*** in which he asked for more time before making a decisive break with Ellénore, but in which he also stated that from that moment onwards his ties with Ellénore were permanently severed. Each of these chapter-endings forcefully points up a crucial development in the story and contains more than the narrator's reflections upon his mental or emotional state (which is for the most part what we are given by the other chapter-endings). Each is the prelude to a new stage in the narrative: to Adolphe's sense of being tied to Ellénore; to the entry in Chapter VII of the Baron de T*** who has received a letter from Adolphe's father; and to the dispatch of a letter that will be used by the Baron to end Adolphe's relationship with Ellénore. The tenth and last chapter then presents the tragic dénouement. What are we to deduce from the shape of the novel with its rhythmic architecture of three 'movements' and final resolution?

Each turns on an error or a misapprehension, but one in which Adolphe firmly believes at the time: first, that Ellénore's love is the greatest gift he could ever receive; then, that his relationship with Ellénore is dead and that his feelings for her are shortly doomed to extinction; finally we read his declaration to the Baron that the ties which bind him to Ellénore can be considered as broken forever. By the end of the novel the reader is able to gauge just how far each of those assessments was mistaken. And yet each statement, though false in one major sense — Ellénore's love brings Adolphe untold misery, his tenderness towards her will not in fact die, and he is never to be free of her presence in his life — is at the same time demonstrated to be true in some other sense. Adolphe does recover his freedom, the relationship is ended for ever, but his desperate loneliness brings the revelation that it is Ellénore's need for him, her absolute dependence upon him that he misses most, the absence of which hurts him deeply. These three moments in the story's progression present us with an Adolphe who anticipates one kind of future situation and then lives to discover a quite different one. They are all highly characteristic of the mode of thought of Benjamin Constant, a man who (according to Sainte-Beuve's well-known anecdote) once told a startled interlocutor: 'Ce que vous dites là est si juste que le contraire est parfaitement vrai', 'what you have just said is so right that the exact opposite is perfectly true'. Constant was obsessively conscious that every argument, every situation had another side to it.

For *Adolphe* is the very novel of *surprise*: it shows that however well prepared human beings may think they are for future eventualities, the unexpected can always overwhelm them. And one of the novel's principal means of throwing new light on experience, of advancing beyond trite explanations towards a more complex and convincing portrayal of human behaviour, is its handling of the paradox. Not only is paradox central to the way the novel is structured: along with irony, it is the most salient feature of its style. Etymologically a paradox, from the Greek *para*, 'against', and *doxa*, 'opinion', is a proposition that runs counter to opinion, to what is generally believed. And in *Adolphe* that *doxa* is always present, assuming many guises, from moral prescriptions and social shibboleths to the everyday assumptions and settled convictions of individuals and groups. A paradox upsets beliefs and expectations and may involve a calling into question of all fixed rules and definitions. Should a paradox gain general acceptance, it will necessarily lose its disruptive power and risk becoming itself a *doxa*: Proust remarked that today's paradox is tomorrow's prejudice. From his youth Constant had a natural aptitude for coining paradoxes, a gift that won him few friends and many critics in Lausanne and elsewhere: he wrote to Mme de Charrière from Lausanne on 9 September 1794, 'Those who tell me I put forward paradoxes in order to show off simply prove that they are unable to find a reply to them.' A paradox may indeed often seem offensive to ordinary common sense – all too frequently the unoriginal derivative of some social *doxa* – when in fact it is merely bypassing common sense in order to reach its ultimate goal, truth.

Adolphe's story presents the reader with paradoxes at every level. It shows how a person can say one thing while meaning another, anticipate one outcome and then discover another, achieve one thing then wish for its opposite; how even a defiant anti-conformist may be tempted by the society whose aridity and artificial values he despises into sacrificing to it that which (though he does not yet realise the fact) is most important to him – indeed how such a man can mistake what

he is most deeply attached to for what he most needs to be
rid of. Things are seldom as they were expected to be, ap-
pearances belie reality: giving and receiving, deprivation and
self-fulfilment, speech and silence are among the many antithetical polarities of human experience that acquire quite
different charges during the course of the story. The path to
happiness which an affair with Ellénore once appeared to be
for Adolphe is the road to misery and self-obliteration. Yet
freedom from servitude to Ellénore turns out to be only worse
misery and a more certain route to self-destruction. Acute
self-awareness, intelligence and lucidity may be of little help
in the pursuit of contentment — they may indeed be an
obstacle. (Constant was well aware of this particular paradox
in his own life and observed on his first marriage to Minna
von Cramm: 'Oh, it is not intelligence that is a weapon: it
is strength of character. I had far more intelligence than
she, and yet she rode roughshod over me.') Society, much
despised for its conventions and simple certainties by
Adolphe and his older woman mentor nevertheless remains
the vehicle of an ancestral wisdom which cannot lightly be set
aside: it is imprudent to ignore the banal rules-of-thumb and
moral guidelines that society has formulated — a society in
which, inevitably, Adolphe must one day play some part. Yet
the received view, the accepted code, the aphorisms and
sententiae current in that society can, when applied to a
specific individual circumstance, simplify, distort, or — as is
the case with the Baron de T***'s confident generalisations
about women like Ellénore — considerably cheapen human
reality. But there is an underlying double paradox here: the
narrator, the older Adolphe, like the 'Publisher' whose letter
closes the novel, has incomparable skill in coining original
and penetrating apothegms. Indeed *Adolphe* must have seemed
to some readers not to be a novel about the problematics
of the maxim but a means by which Constant delivered
himself of a large number of such formulations. The truth
surely is, however, that *Adolphe* establishes a continual
counterpoint between on the one hand the narrator's personal
discovery of certain paradigms for making sense of existence

and on the other the exposure and dismantling of the discredited universal rules and absolutes of others, and perhaps of the narrator's former self.

The effect of paradox is surprise and even shock resulting from the revelation of that which is odd, unusual or inexplicable in human experience. Several great French novels before *Adolphe* had been characterised by a strong element of the paradoxical. In *Les Liaisons dangereuses* (1782) Laclos had created the figure of an attractive ruthless libertine, Valmont, who in the process of his scheming and manoeuvres to seduce the pious Mme de Tourvel comes to feel the passion which he has at first only pretended to experience. In *Adolphe* one of the most frequently recurring adjectives is *bizarre*, and in the course of the novel the continual discovery of strange, disturbing and occasionally wryly amusing truths about human experience calls into question a wide range of accepted ideas and attitudes. This leads also to a many-sided inquiry into words and definitions, their power and their relationship to the ever-changing life of the emotions. The story ends with the statement in Ellénore's letter that Adolphe's actions have hurt her less than his words − a troubling final paradox which calls into question the commonplace belief that language is essentially harmless: here, as in *Les Liaisons dangereuses*, words have the power to kill.

Words and feelings

Adolphe is an exploration not only of the paradoxes of situation but also of language. It offers an extraordinarily sophisticated investigation of the relationship between changing feelings and the language available to define them and plot their transformations. In the course of the story a number of key words appear to become, as it were, unstable and their meaning to shift between positive and negative senses, between one thing and its very opposite. In some languages certain words can commonly have a double, ambiguous or undecidable meaning: Plato pointed to the word *pharmakon* in Greek as having two opposite meanings, both 'poison' and 'cure'. In English the noun 'sanction', for example, can mean both 'authorisation' and 'penalty'. Now in *Adolphe* a sequence of complex situations brings out not only the contradictory quality of characters' thoughts and emotions but also the disquietingly ambiguous implications latent in the words which express them: *lien*, like its English equivalents 'bond' and 'tie', has in the novel both the generally positive meaning implied in, say, the 'bond' between parent and child or the 'marriage tie', and the negative sense which relates it to bondage and constraint. The word is a miniature oxymoron, a point at which the incongruities and contradictions of experience are brought forcefully together. But in a less obvious way the noun *sacrifice* and the verb *sacrifier* also oscillate between more positive and more negative meanings as the novel progresses. The subtlety with which in each new context the word is made to render a slightly different reverberation can perhaps best be likened to the fine gradations of sound and tone produced by a finger when it strikes a piano key at different speeds and with varying pressure.

The word *lien* is, as I indicated, an example of how Constant allows the different shades of meaning contained in a word to reflect the changing human situation in *Adolphe*. It is one of the most frequently occurring and significant nouns in the novel, and first appears in the crucially important first chapter where it is placed quite deliberately in juxtaposition to Adolphe's account of the constraint he felt with his father and its effect on his behaviour. The lack of easy and open discussion between them drove Adolphe in upon himself; it made it hard for him to show his feelings or share his plans with others; it made him solitary in his habits, uneasy in company and flippant in conversation. Then the word makes its appearance:

Il en résulta en même temps un désir ardent d'indépendance, une grande impatience des liens dont j'étais environné, une terreur invincible d'en former de nouveaux. (Ch. I, p. 111)

(This gave rise at the same time to a burning desire for independence in me, considerable impatience with the ties which surrounded me, and an insurmountable panic at the thought of forming new ones.)

This sense of being hemmed in and suffocated as the result of ties — social and family connections — and the fear of contracting any more are attributed to his unsatisfactory relationship with his father. *Lien* has here a deeply negative charge acquired by its association with a relationship that has failed. The word next occurs when Adolphe in a frenzy of desire for Ellénore threatens her with all sorts of consequences if she does not allow him to call on her the following morning:

> j'abandonne mon pays, ma famille et mon père, je romps tous mes liens, j'abjure tous mes devoirs, et je vais, n'importe où, finir au plus tôt une vie que vous vous plaisez à empoisonner.(Ch. II, pp. 127–8)

> (I shall abandon my country, my family and my father, I shall sever all ties, abjure all obligations and go no matter where to end a life which you take pleasure in destroying.)

The reader naturally asks whether Adolphe has changed, whether he is quite the same man to speak positively thus of such *liens*: indeed he is shortly not to be his normal self when briefly intoxicated by the passion he has thought himself into, but at this point, at the end of Chapter II, there is an element of deceit in his words, the deceit of a maladroit but determined seducer. In Chapter III it is Ellénore, fatigued by the demands he makes upon her for some tangible sign of affection, who contemplates breaking the *lien* between them, and in the same chapter the general opinion of polite society is that the Comte de P*** could have formed 'des liens plus honorables' — again *lien* is exhibited in its positive sense: that of the conventional and approved union of marriage. But to be able to appreciate such a *lien* is not in Adolphe's character, or so he believes: what he does experience, most acutely, is being tied to the woman he once desired; and the knell on his short-lived happiness is sounded by a sentence which carries an ominous echo of his most fundamental fear:

> Ellénore était sans doute un vif plaisir dans mon existence, mais elle n'était plus un but: elle était devenue un lien.   (Ch. IV, p. 140)

> (Certainly Ellénore was a keen source of pleasure in my life, but she was no longer a goal towards which I was striving: she had become a tie.)

There is a crushing finality to the statement, and from this
point on in the story *lien* comes to represent the burden of
Adolphe's relationship with Ellénore, with its demands and
obligations:

la difficulté de la situation, la certitude d'un avenir qui devait nous
séparer, peut-être je ne sais quelle révolte contre un lien qu'il m'était
impossible de briser, me dévoraient intérieurement.

(Ch. V, pp. 152–3)

(the difficulty of our position, the certainty of a future which would
see our separation, perhaps a kind of revolt in me against a tie it was
impossible for me to break, all were tormenting me.)

Lien has become an instrument of bondage, it denies him his
freedom. Yet Adolphe has, it would seem, no scruple about
using the word in its positive sense in a rhetorical attempt to
reassure Ellénore at the end of Chapter V when he tells her,
after she has spent a night in anguish, that they are to leave
together and that he knows he cannot be happy without her:
'je voulais lui consacrer ma vie et nous unir par tous les genres
de liens' (p. 159) ('I wanted to devote my life to her and bind her
to myself by every possible bond'). Ellénore is not deceived
and sees through to his real feelings, telling him that it is not
love he feels, only pity. Within a few lines, at the beginning
of Chapter VI, Adolphe is resentful at his father's clumsy
stratagem which, by forcing him to flee the country with
Ellénore, has succeeded not in cutting him free of his bonds
but in tightening them ('resserré mes liens', p. 160). They
become in his mind like chains which he is forced to drag
behind him, once the Baron de T*** has adroitly planted in
his mind the idea that he may one day find a calm and stable
relationship:

Je réfléchis au repos, à la considération, à l'indépendance même que
m'offrirait un sort pareil; car les liens que je traînais depuis si
longtemps me rendaient plus dépendant mille fois que n'aurait pu le
faire une union reconnue et constatée.   (Ch. VII, p. 174)

(I mused on the tranquillity, on the favourable reputation, even on
the independence which such a change in my life would bring. For
the fetters which I had been trailing behind me for so long made me
infinitely more dependent than a publicly recognised and legitimate
union could ever have done.)

The fact that Adolphe experiences his connection with Ellénore as a kind of shackle weighing upon him is subtly linked to the notion with which *lien* was first associated in Chapter I, that of his desperate need to be independent; perhaps it is a signal that events are moving towards a crisis. Adolphe now becomes, despite himself, guilty of duplicity, concealing from Ellénore the Baron's intention of separating him from her, yet at the same time giving the Baron a false impression that he is on the point of breaking all ties ('prêt à briser mes liens', p. 190) with Ellénore. But the Baron is too able and single-minded a diplomat to be satisfied merely with vague hints: when Adolphe puts in writing that henceforth all connection between himself and his mistress can be considered to have ended forever ('mes liens avec Ellénore comme brisés pour jamais', p. 193), the Baron ensures that Ellénore learns of the document, with, as it turns out, fatal results.

Now a change occurs in Adolphe's use of the word *lien*. In his frantic efforts to persuade Ellénore to live, he asks her, this time with every appearance of meaning what he says:

nos âmes ne sont-elles pas enchaînées l'une à l'autre par mille liens que rien ne peut rompre?   (Ch. X, p. 197)

(Are our souls not held to one another by a thousand ties which nothing can sever?)

At her death, he records,

Je sentis le dernier lien se rompre, et l'affreuse réalité se placer à jamais entre elle et moi   (Ch. X, p. 203)

(I felt the last bond between us snap and dreadful reality coming forever between her and myself),

and the terrible paradox of his situation is driven home in the next sentence which brings together all the connotations of chains and servitude which have attached themselves to the word *lien* in the course of the novel:

Combien elle me pesait, cette liberté que j'avais tant regrettée!
                                                    (Ch. X, pp. 203–4)

(How heavily that freedom I had longed to regain now weighed upon me!)

It is left to Ellénore in her letter to Adolphe to bring home
to him the lacerating tragic irony of his position by asking
him from beyond the grave:

Par quelle pitié bizarre n'osez-vous rompre un lien qui vous pèse, et
déchirez-vous l'être malheureux près de qui votre pitié vous retient?
(Ch. X, p. 204)

(What strange kind of pity is it that prevents you from breaking a
chain which weighs heavily upon you and makes you torment the
hapless creature your pity will not let you leave?)

A still more complex pattern emerges from a study of
sacrifice and *sacrifier* and their significance at various points
in the novel. Ellénore's capacity for uncomplaining self-
sacrifice was one of the factors which placed the Comte de
P*** in her debt when he was trying to recover his property
(Ch. II, p. 120), but Adolphe, at the beginning of the story
no doubt full of admiration for the ideal image of the woman
he is to fall in love with, later comes to experience another
side of that quality in her. In Chapter IV Ellénore's power to
make a sacrifice of herself increases *her* attachment to *him* —
a nice, ironic touch since conventional wisdom might suggest
that it would increase *his* attachment to *her* — and her pro-
digality with her sacrifices is such that they become a burden
on the one who is forced to 'accept' them (the verb *accepter*
is used on no fewer than four occasions for what is being
required of Adolphe). The noun *sacrifice* and the verb
sacrifier are, when taken together, an invaluable pointer to a
paradoxical aspect of the novel's meaning. The two words
are, as it were, held up and turned in the light to display their
lesser known, indeed commonly unsuspected facets. For in
the world which Constant creates, Ellénore's sacrifices are a
far from simple matter. To the casual observer they may
appear to be freely generous acts; a La Rochefoucauld, intent
on showing how love of self permeates every human trans-
action, might see them as self-serving — in Maxim 263 he
wrote 'What is called generosity is more often than not only
the vanity of giving, which brings us more pleasure than the
thing we give.' But Constant goes further: *of course* our feelings and motives are, as the novel suggests at one point,

complex mixtures, and Ellénore's contain elements of both
the selfish and the selfless. She appears sincere in what she
does, but the gamble she has taken is a considerable one and the
sacrifices she makes may be her quite conscious way of binding
Adolphe more securely to her. But, however that may be, what
distinguishes Constant's novel is what must surely be an un-
paralleled exploration of the effect of a sacrifice on the person
in favour of whom it is made, the supposed *beneficiary*. For
Ellénore's sacrifices create such a fund of obligation and
embarrassed gratitude on Adolphe's part that she effectively
dominates him through them: they are equivalent to what an-
thropologists call a *potlatch*, a lavish gift which secures her
hold – what the narrator calls her *empire bizarre* (Chapter IV)
– over him. That *empire* is *bizarre* precisely because
Adolphe's personality is such as to make him uniquely
vulnerable to Ellénore's gestures, aware as he is of how much
she has given up for him, and having a hyperacute sense of her
vulnerability in a society which would ostracise her if he were to
abandon her. Ellénore gives up the things she wants less, in
order to have the one thing she really wants, to live with
Adolphe. The irony is that Adolphe too is making a sacrifice,
perhaps the greater one: he is forgoing what is most essential to
him, his autonomy, his freedom of action, but, to add to his
suffering, Ellénore's sacrifices put him permanently at a moral
disadvantage – and they are repeated throughout the story.
Imposed on him and unasked for, they create in Adolphe a
moral conflict that brings him to the verge of despair:

J'étais touché, mais au désespoir du nouveau sacrifice que me faisait
Ellénore.   (Ch. VI, p. 162)

(I was moved, but in despair, at this new sacrifice which Ellénore
had made on my behalf.)

And hence the paradox: what seems perhaps the very essence
of selflessness leads in practice to the imposition of one person's will on another and to an infringement of the integrity
of that second party whose interests are not properly con-
sulted – or are assumed to coincide with those of the one
making the sacrifice.

Through raising the problem of who is making the greater sacrifice in the situation, *Adolphe* leads us to ask a still more fundamental question: what exactly is love? For if Ellénore truly loves Adolphe, if she is genuinely concerned about *his* best interests and happiness, ought she not to make the one sacrifice which she is not prepared to make, the one which would give Adolphe his freedom? The fact that she is unwilling to relinquish possession of him and that her repeated sacrifices have the effect of blackmailing him shows no less tellingly than might a Racine tragedy the degree of self-interest involved in love. The three occasions when Adolphe refers to his own sacrifices are thrown into strong relief, and the Baron's indirect allusion to his position is nicely calculated to capitalise on the young man's resentment:

tel homme qui pense de bonne foi s'immoler au désespoir qu'il a causé, ne se sacrifie dans le fait qu'aux illusions de sa propre vanité.
(Ch. VII, p. 170)

(a man who thinks in good faith that he is sacrificing himself to the despair which he has caused is in reality only sacrificing himself to the illusions of his own vanity.)

Interestingly it is Adolphe's sacrifices that Constant underlines in a letter dated 26 February 1807 to Sophie Gay (which was published for the first time in 1963). The women who have heard him read his novel or have read it themselves

disent toutes qu'il devrait aimer, comme si aimer, et surtout aimer toujours, était chose simple et facile; et parce que le pauvre diable n'aime plus, on ne lui sait aucun gré de ce qu'il fait ou de ce qu'il sacrifie. Voilà comme vous êtes toutes, légères quand on vous aime, ingrates pour toutes les marques de dévouement qu'on vous donne quand on ne vous aime plus.   (Quoted in *Adolphe*, p. 263)

(all say that he ought to love her, as if loving someone, and above all loving someone forever, was an easy and simple thing. And because the poor devil no longer loves her, no one is grateful to him for what he does or what he sacrifices. That's the way you women always are, fickle when a man loves you, ungrateful for all the evidence of his devotion when he no longer loves you.)

It is worth noting too that the words *dévoué* and *dévouement*, 'devoted' and 'devotion' are fairly evenly distributed between Ellénore and Adolphe himself in the novel.

It would be easy to add to the examples I have given. The point which I wish to emphasise is the capacity words have to slip their moorings and drift by degrees, and sometimes imperceptibly, a surprising distance from their original starting-place; or rather, that it is the events and experiences of the story which make words yield a different sense as the drama unfolds. Self-giving can become a form of tyranny to its recipient, a love relationship can degenerate into a form of enslavement for one party to it; freedom can rob the person who has longed for independence of all purpose in life, of all desire to go on living: such arresting discoveries as these — and there are many in the course of the story — and the process by which they are arrived at are not merely incidental in *Adolphe*. Clearly they constitute essential parts of the novel's conceptual structure and can lead us towards an interpretation. For there is nothing merely ingenious in the way Constant handles paradox and the irony to which it lends impetus: his aim is an intensely serious one, the presentation of an insoluble and tragic human dilemma.

Tradition and originality

Despite superficial resemblances to the *moraliste* and maxim-writer La Rochefoucauld — and in life, as one could have guessed, he coined brilliant epigrams with ease — Constant is with *Adolphe* quintessentially a novelist, and the contradictory and contrary nature of human existence receives in the novel a powerful dramatic embodiment in narrative. The opening paragraph of *Adolphe* is subtly ironic in several ways, as befits what Alison Fairlie in a well-chosen phrase calls 'that most quietly disruptive of all French novels' (Fairlie, p. 3). Critics have frequently pointed out that the story of a seducer who is a little too wise before the event, who thinks himself immune to the emotion he is trying to inspire in a woman and who is not, links *Adolphe* directly with the central figure of Laclos' *Les Liaisons dangereuses* (1782). What makes *Adolphe* different, it need hardly be said, is that the story is concerned principally with what happens *after* Adolphe's passion for his mistress has left him. However, what has not been examined is the similarity between the opening of Constant's novel and that of a famous 'confessional' novel which was familiar to both Constant and his readers, the Abbé Prévost's *Manon Lescaut* (1731), the tale of an austere and intelligent young man who falls desperately in love with an amoral girl and who, in order to satisfy her appetite for pleasure and luxuries, is led into the world of low-life Paris, to commit a series of crimes culminating in murder. (In a similar way to *Adolphe*, Prévost's novel begins with a typically eighteenth-century framing foreword followed by an account of the circumstances in which the narrator came to tell his story: it is not impossible that Constant was to some degree influenced by these.) The narrative proper begins:

> I was seventeen and finishing my philosophy studies at Amiens where my parents, who belong to one of the best families in P., had sent me. I led so well-ordered and upright an existence that my teachers cited me as an example to the rest of the college. Not that I made any extraordinary effort to deserve their praise, but by nature I am quiet and good-humoured: I applied myself to my studies out of inclination . . . My good birth, the success of my studies and my general appearance had brought me to the attention of the respectable families in the town and had won me their esteem . . . When the holidays came round, I was preparing to return to the house of my father who had promised to send me shortly to the Academy.

At this point the Chevalier des Grieux meets Manon Lescaut and, to the dismay of his father, begins a hectic affair which will ruin his life and end with Manon's death in America.

When contemporary readers of *Adolphe* saw the first page of the novel, their expectation could not but be that it would be like what they already knew. But, as we know, it is not: it is only superficially like *Manon* and then only at the outset – Des Grieux's academic success, his father's (premature) satisfaction, the prospect of further achievements lead on to his hopeless and indestructible passion for what the world judges an unsuitable mistress. It was entirely characteristic of Constant's critical and provocative intelligence to delight in doing the unexpected, the unthought-of. And in *Adolphe* he set wholly new parameters for the novel by taking his reader into a territory which was seldom explored, that which lay on the far side of a love affair. It is a story which quite deliberately continues and develops where others leave off, and one which had grown out of his own personal experience.

The opening page confronts us with another curious feature. That *Adolphe* owes much to two French literary traditions, that of the *roman d'analyse*, the novel of close psychological analysis, and that of the *roman libertin*, the novel of seduction popularised by Crébillon *fils* and brought to its apogee by Laclos, is beyond doubt. It is further generally agreed by commentators that *Adolphe* is the work of a 'kindred spirit' to writers in the 'tradition of the great French *moralistes'* (the description given by W. G. Moore who added that Constant was 'surely among [La Rochefoucauld's] perceptive readers'). Yet, curiously, although much has been written about Ellénore's Polish origins and their possible significance in the story, it seems often to have gone unnoticed that the principal protagonist himself is very clearly a young *German* intellectual. The psychological analysis in *Adolphe* is uncompromisingly sharp and very French, but the stress which the narrative lays on subjective experience, on Adolphe's inner life, on the processes of his thought, on his memories, day-dreams, perplexities and periods of lassitude as well as on his acute sensibility and tendency to melancholia, must surely mirror the fact that when *Adolphe* was written – and still more by the time it was published – Germany had become synonymous with the philosophy of mind and the metaphysical speculations of a Kant or a Schelling, with the self-conscious sufferings of Goethe's Werther, and with the individualism and rebellion against authority of every kind associated with the writers of the *Sturm und Drang*. As early as 1794 Constant had come, in spite of himself, to prize German thinkers and historians ('I find them infinitely superior to the French and the English. They are more learned, more impartial, more exact, a little too diffuse, but nearly always judicious, truthful, courageous and moderate', he told Mme de Charrière on 7 June 1794 (*O.C.*,

IV, p. 458)), and in his later years he became, one might almost say, half-German by virtue of his researches on religion which had instilled in him a profound admiration for the seriousness, thoroughness and precision of German scholarship. Adolphe's narrative, with its convincing account of the dynamics of subjective life, and its anatomising of the mind's perception of the world and interaction with other subjectivities, exhibits the preoccupations of a typically German intellect and sensibility of the period. The fact that, as we know, many of these concerns and attitudes were also Constant's own does not diminish the achievement of a wholly plausible character for the setting that is evoked. Critics of 1816 were, to this extent at least, perceptive in detecting a Germanic flavour not only in the novel's style, which was severely criticised by some ('bizarre and affected turns of phrase', 'cosmopolitan style', 'Germanified language'), but also in its thought: the reviewers of *Le Constitutionnel* in particular related the novel to the new literary doctrines of Romanticism, seeing in it a connection with August Wilhelm Schlegel's interest in the relationship between 'the phenomena of the mental world and the phenomena of the visible world' (*Adolphe*, pp. 284–95).

However, there is perhaps still more to the novel's singularity than this. The form of *Adolphe*, quite exceptional in its strict control, and the evident disproportion between its length – no more than a hundred pages or so in most editions – and the depth of experience it conveys, have always seemed to set it apart from other French novels. This may not have been simply because the story needed to be short enough for Constant to read aloud in a salon, or even because *Adolphe* was the product of an intellect more used to the logical rigour and concision of philosophical inquiry. When Constant wrote *Adolphe* he possibly had in mind a narrative model which, by the beginning of the nineteenth century, and largely as a result of the example of Goethe (*Unterhaltungen deutscher Ausgewanderten*, *Conversations of German Emigrés*, 1795) and the aesthetic theories of Friedrich Schlegel, was becoming an art form whose strict exigencies had no real counterpart in

French fiction: I am thinking of the German *Novelle* which in length lay somewhere between the novel and the short story. Following the distant example of the stories in Boccaccio's *Decameron*, the *Novelle* tended to appear within a *Rahmen* or narrative framework; it might, for example, be told by one member of a group of people staying at a country house in order to entertain the others; it dealt succinctly with one central problem (in Goethe frequently a moral conflict), presented only a limited number of characters and kept circumstantial detail to a minimum; in the course of the anecdote it brought to light something unusual or strange, perhaps some hitherto neglected aspect of human nature, but set in the recognisable world of everyday social life; it might contain a *Wendepunkt* or 'turning-point', an ironic twist or perhaps a conclusion which, though logically coherent, was nevertheless surprising (or, as Goethe said, 'unheard-of').

If we are to believe his Preface to the third edition of *Adolphe*, Constant originally composed his 'Anecdote' (the word appears in the title) during a stay in the country and with the intention of convincing some friends 'of the possibility of lending a certain interest to a novel in which the number of characters would be reduced to two and in which the situation would be the same throughout'. (The challenging paradox of being required to provide sufficient novelty and variety within an essentially restricted and static situation must have greatly appealed to him.) The narrative of *Adolphe* is set in a wider framework, being preceded by a 'Publisher's Note' which describes the Publisher's meeting with a stranger in an Italian inn − in the event the stranger becomes the story-teller − who falls ill, is cured and leaves, and then the subsequent discovery of a casket containing the manuscript; the narrative is followed by the two closing letters which offer differing interpretations of Adolphe's story. The unity of *Adolphe* is assured by its concentration on one central event and problem, Adolphe's love affair with Ellénore and its aftermath; the novel's source of interest is the psychology of the two principal characters, the investigation of which also throws light on unsuspected facets of human behaviour; it has several ironic twists which are a direct consequence of Adolphe's seduction of Ellénore — an event which has unforeseen repercussions that culminate in Ellénore's illness and death and Adolphe's wretchedness.

Those characteristics which distinguish *Adolphe* from so many other French novels — its studied restraint and concentration on the essential; its relative brevity and reduction of the physical and natural world to symbolic form or to spare but telling notation; its narrator, who directly recounts and throws light on his past experiences but whose testimony is differently refracted by two critical outside observers at the close; the sense of an inevitably tragic outcome which is established before the story proper can begin by the 'Publisher's Note'; perhaps even the fact that no character is given a full surname but only a Christian name or title (a feature which has puzzled literary historians, such a usage being largely out of fashion in France since the mid eighteenth century, as Delbouille points out in his edition, p. 41) — all these elements which taken in isolation might seem to have a purely French pedigree, in combination suggest the influence of the German *Novelle*. If my conjecture is correct we may have in *Adolphe* a particularly happy conjunction: a story whose hallmark is something quite new on this scale in French fiction and for which the appropriate word would be *Innerlichkeit* — inwardness, intense introspection, the pursuit of fine definition in the exploration of changing states of mind and feeling — and a narrative form peculiarly appropriate for expressing this content with the maximum concentration, both features of course bringing inescapably to mind the German milieu to which the central character belongs. In *Adolphe* we may have, in short, the paradox of a German *Novelle* written in French.

At this point a word of caution is necessary: *Adolphe* is not without a number of specifically French literary antecedents, as Paul Delbouille indicated in his important study *Genèse, structure et destin d''Adolphe'* (Paris, 1971). We have already noted echoes of *Manon Lescaut* and *Les Liaisons dangereuses*, but most important in connection with the features of the novel I have listed above is Mme de Charrière's *Caliste*, a work which pre-dates Mme de Staël's *Corinne* (by two decades) and Chateaubriand's *René*, works often cited by critics as having possibly exercised an influence on Constant when he wrote *Adolphe*. Not only does *Caliste* have something of the admirable compression of Constant's masterpiece, it has a hero and heroine who in some respects resemble Adolphe and Ellénore; it too is set in a wider narrative framework and even maintains the old-fashioned convention of suppressing surnames. What is more, the narrator William's account of his treatment of Caliste, sombre and meditative in tone, at times comes close to Adolphe's and contains flashes of insight – in that 'limpid and terse style', as Paul Debouille characterises Mme de Charrière's manner (*Adolphe*, p. 42) – which are similarly penetrating. We shall have reason to return to *Caliste* at a later point, but it must be said at once of Mme de Charrière's novel that although it does to some extent look like an embryonic version of *Adolphe*, it lacks the power and compelling profundity of Constant's work, and it conveys considerably less detail of experience.

To summarise then: *Adolphe* appears closest to the French *moralistes* of the seventeenth century, in particular La Rochefoucauld, and to the tradition of the *roman d'analyse* established by Mme de Lafayette's *La Princesse de Clèves* if one considers the complexity of its psychological analyses; its opening and its theme appear to be a knowing and ironic echo of, respectively, *Manon Lescaut* and *Les Liaisons dangereuses*; for a certain tone and mood, and for elegant and lapidary concentration, *Adolphe* seems to some degree indebted to Mme de Charrière's *Caliste*; its exploration of the inner life of an isolated individual would seem to reflect a trend in German literature since Goethe's *Werther*, and its form that of the *Novelle*. It would not be difficult to extend the list of possible borrowings: critics have drawn analogies with the tragedies of Racine, so much admired by Constant (the inexorable logic of its progression, the limited vocabulary), and in particular with *Bérénice*, where the challenge to the dramatist, as Racine stated in his *Préface*,

was not unlike that facing Constant: 'toute l'invention con-
siste à faire quelque chose de rien', the inventiveness required
of the tragedian is that of being able to make something out
of nothing. For *Bérénice* is a story in which very little happens
except the heart-searching which precedes the Emperor
Titus's reluctant dismissal of his mistress Bérénice. Literary
history must have its due. So too, however, must the
originality, polish, and sheer intellectual vigour of Constant
as he transforms personal experience and literary reminiscence into something that stands quite apart from the other
(not infrequently lesser) works of art with which one might be
tempted to compare it. Paul Delbouille, whose great study
has been *Adolphe* and its literary antecedents, is aware of the
danger of making a highly original novel falsely cohere with
what has gone before, and in his edition of the novel points
to the unusualness of its theme and tone among French novels
(pp. 38–9).

Chapter 5

Character and circumstance

Father and son

A detailed examination of the first three chapters of *Adolphe* reveals with what extraordinary care Constant prepares the reader for the thematic centre of the work, the impasse of Adolphe's relationship with Ellénore, and how he sets before us in rapid succession the facts of character and situation which will lead directly or indirectly to the final climax of the story. In his Journal entry for 26 August 1804 Constant had singled out the way Friedrich Schlegel set before the reader the personality and background of Julius, the central figure in his German novel *Lucinde*, as being one of the most praiseworthy parts of the book. Schlegel's heading, 'Lehr-jahre der Männlichkeit', 'years of apprenticeship for manhood', would indeed be appropriate for the opening pages of *Adolphe*, for these constitute a rich matrix out of which the leitmotifs of the novel will slowly unfold and grow.

The first paragraph of the older Adolphe's narrative is full of ironies and very knowingly wrought, drawing the reader's eye to one of the key elements in the plot, the theme of ambition, associated from the beginning with the collision between two personalities, those of Adolphe and his father. The second sentence of the narrative, 'L'intention de mon père . . .', 'My father's intention was that . . .', needs to be understood with the rest of the paragraph which follows it: after achieving success at university, Adolphe has raised his father's hopes to the extent that, after sending his son on the Grand Tour, he intends that he will one day succeed him as Minister to the Elector of ***. That paternal 'intention' with its slight undertone of menace casts a shadow forwards across the novel, for it will ultimately bring about the dénouement, precipitated by the zeal of the Baron de T*** on behalf of

Adolphe's father. In this first paragraph the older Adolphe surmises how his father must have seen him at the outset, that is as an academic success: he was ignorant of − or chose to ignore − the other Adolphe who was leading a life of dissipation and making his way by dint of unremitting hard work. (During his 'night walk' in Chapter VII, p. 173, the 'travail assez opiniâtre' and 'vie très dissipée' are echoed in Adolphe's bitterly ironic reflections on the worldly success of former fellow-students on whom he had once looked with disdain, success achieved thanks to *their* subsequent unremitting hard work, 'travail opiniâtre', and − most painful of all − their 'vie régulière' which contrasts with his 'irregular life' with Ellénore.) There is a gulf in understanding between the returning student and his father, and the self-critical *probablement*, '*probably* much exaggerated hopes', establishes that distance which is amplified upon in the third and succeeding paragraphs of the first chapter. There is, finally, a dark irony in the plan that Adolphe should visit 'those countries most worthy of note in Europe', given the glimpse we have already gained of him in Italy: indeed Adolphe *is* destined to travel, but, as he tells the Publisher, because of the experiences which his narrative recounts, it has become a matter of supreme indifference to him whether he is in one place or another (p. 107).

The second paragraph takes up the idea of misunderstanding between two different temperaments which was first introduced by the placing of the 'probably'. Repeating the word *espérances*, the 'hopes' or 'expectations' of Adolphe's father, it recounts how these led him to condone his son's occasional youthful indiscretions and to protect him from any unfortunate consequences which might arise from such behaviour. There are several important points here: whatever the excesses of youth referred to may be − and we are no doubt meant to infer that sexual promiscuity is one of them − by his indulgence Adolphe's father reveals the belief which will condition his and society's reactions to the affair with Ellénore: that all manner of licence is permissible before a young man finally marries and settles down to a position in life.

Thereafter — outwardly at least — strict conformity with conventional standards of behaviour will be required of him. There is, too, the obvious dramatic irony (in the light of what is to come) that Adolphe's father by his excessively generous treatment of his son has done little to instil in him any sense of responsibility, a fact which makes it not unlikely that he will do something as rash as to seduce Ellénore; so that in the long term the son could be seen to suffer through the father's generosity. This point is brought out strongly when Adolphe's father determines to have Ellénore banished from the town where she is living with Adolphe (Ch. V) and tells him, 'I have always left you a great deal of freedom and have never wished to know anything about your love affairs, but it is not proper for you at your age to have a publicly acknowledged mistress.' This characteristically blunt and somewhat ill-judged attempt to bring his son to heel risks having the opposite effect, as Adolphe tells him, of binding him to Ellénore for ever. The father's action comes too late to reverse the damage his earlier laxity brought about. And finally there is a parallel here less often noticed than it ought to be: Adolphe is allowed a degree of liberty, perhaps unwisely in the light of subsequent events, which is not dissimilar to that which the Comte de P*** allows, no less unwisely, to Ellénore. For, as early as this in the narrative, Constant is at pains to build up subtly the parallels as well as the contrasts between the personalities of Adolphe and Ellénore and the situations in which they find themselves.

There are a considerable number of such clues which the observant reader is undoubtedly expected to note and to recognise when they recur at other points in the story. They are part of the novel's highly elaborate network of echoes, in which motifs, phrases, parallels or half-parallels reappear in the story and produce in the reader's mind the satisfying effect of rhyme or para-rhyme or the equally pleasing sensation of contrast which results from a reversal of expectation. One of these parallels can be found in the third paragraph of Chapter I. There is, we are told, a lack of tenderness between father and son, and Adolphe characterises his father's treatment of him as 'plutôt noble et généreuse que tendre' ('generous and noble rather than tender'), anticipating the later description of Ellénore's attachment to her children as 'plutôt passionné que tendre' ('passionate rather than tender'). Adolphe, who looks to his father for *tendresse* and meets with only a formal and correct or, worse, a coolly ironic response, is forced in upon himself. He will later look for some relief from the opposite extreme in behaviour, from Ellénore's passionate intensity in her love for him, but will seldom find that gentle warmth, that tenderness which he seeks. And when he does find it, as one might expect in such a story, it only torments him the more, as for example when Ellénore nurses him after his duel and intensifies his sense of guilt and remorse for no longer being able to return her passion (Ch. V), or at the end, when throughout her illness she shows unwavering tenderness towards him (Ch. X). Given her personality, traits of which are aggravated by her precarious position in society, Ellénore behaves towards Adolphe in a way which – and we are meant to register the parallel – is analogous to her treatment of her children when she was living with the Comte de P***. In Chapter IV she frets if Adolphe is away for two hours, an observation which recalls the anguish she felt if her children were 'away from her for an hour' (Ch. II). The relationship cross-links with an earlier and formative relationship where there was no tenderness: Ellénore's actions will have a no less alienating effect upon the young man than has his father's treatment of him. A further intriguing point: the 'gratitude and respect' with which Adolphe responds to his father's treatment of him are matched exactly by the gratitude and respect he feels after Ellénore gives herself to him: can this be accidental? At all events the constraint and lack of openness that will shortly exist between Adolphe and Ellénore are, as we shall see, directly or indirectly the legacy of Adolphe's relationship with his father.

La timidité

During the first two decades of his life Adolphe learns to hide his true feelings, which he knows would be met by his father's condescending smile or sarcasm. He withdraws into uncommunicative isolation. Yet in the differences between them one can detect an ironic similarity: the father looks down on the son's youthful enthusiasms; the son, full of adolescent passion and energy, looks with condescension on the mundane world around him. Adolphe himself is shortly to become nothing less than a 'cool and caustic observer' of the absurdities of polite society, and to suffer the consequences. The lengthy description of the respective character traits of father and son has as its purpose the artistic justification of how Adolphe will react during the emotional turmoil of the later chapters. It contains a plausible measure of 'like father, like son', demonstrating how inherited characteristics are acted upon by experience — in this case the actual circumstances of the difficult relationship between father and son — so that aspects of Adolphe's personality have been exaggerated or displaced in ways which will have a direct bearing on the plot.

The detailed commentary on the *timidité* of father and son performs several vital functions connected with the narrative we are about to read: first, by remarks of the 'at the time I had not yet realised' kind it lends a certain depth in time to the story, and this impression is carefully sustained throughout the length of the novel; then, since *timidité* denotes not merely shyness or awkwardness but a more general inability to communicate one's feelings, it prepares the way for many variations in the novel on the theme of the power or, alternatively, the inadequacy of language. At a more literal level the excursus on being unable to share one's deepest feelings with another person anticipates, almost word for word, the wry comedy of the gauche seducer in Chapter II ('But I was held back by my unconquerable timidity: everything I was about to say died on my lips, or ended differently from how I had intended'). It prefigures, in that same chapter, Adolphe's ability to express in a letter what he has not the courage to tell Ellénore face to face (how ironically like his father!), and also the later handicap of being unable to tell her the terrible secret that he is no longer in love with her. (There the character-trait joins forces with another secondary to it, disarray and loss of resolve at the sight of another person's face, a characteristic of which we shall see more presently.) In Chapter X Adolphe tries inadequately to sum up what Ellénore genuinely means to him and then snatches hope from her by stuttering that 'one day, perhaps' he will leave her: his words, as well as betraying his perplexity and weakness, perhaps also look back to the 'mots vagues', the 'general terms' referred to here in Chapter I apropos of his father's reserve, and are a reminder of the tragic distortion of what one is trying to say that such timidity can engender. Finally this account of *timidité* and its effects looks forwards to the posthumous letter of Ellénore with its reproach about Adolphe's words being so much more hurtful than his deeds. One could ask, too, whether the oblique way in which, in Chapter IX, Adolphe speaks to the Baron of the difficulty of making a final break with a woman (itself echoing his vague fulminations against women in general and their *empire* over men in Chapter V) is not a deliberate reminiscence of the 'more or less bitter irony' to which the person unable to communicate the full depth and complexity of his emotions is likely to resort. Yet Adolphe's father, outwardly so cold, thinks it is his *son* who is lacking in affection, a state of affairs resulting from the failure of communication between them: this surely prefigures Ellénore's sense of hurt at her failure to understand fully Adolphe's complex feelings towards her, a failure deriving from an analogous lack of communication between the couple.

Not only did Adolphe become withdrawn: we are told that he contracted the habit of never sharing his plans with other people, counting only on himself for their execution. He came to consider the interest, advice and help of others as a hindrance and an obstacle. Once again one notes the irony whereby the father who will so disapprove of his son's liaison with Ellénore becomes, by his son's account, partly responsible for the 'solitary plan' the son is shortly to carry through, the seduction of Ellénore — responsible because of the way he has treated him. But in the light of subsequent events there is a further depth of tragic irony concealed here, an irony so exquisite that it approaches the kind of dark wit which Constant's early mentor Mme de Charrière would have appreciated. The self-sufficient Adolphe, who by Chapter IX through self-sacrifice and abnegation has achieved a difficult equilibrium in his relationship with Ellénore, is drawn gently and with infinite skill into the confidence of a man whom he yet knows to be 'un vieux ministre dont l'âme était usée' (p. 189), 'an old, worldly wise and blasé diplomat'. In fact Adolphe seeks out the man's company and is moved by the interest the Baron de T*** shows in his talents, abilities and possible future career. The irony, of course, is that if Adolphe had indeed trusted the instinct of self-reliance which he had developed as a consequence of his lack of easy communication with his father, he would never have fallen into the Baron's — and hence his father's — trap. This is underlined by the narrator's rueful apostrophe to the reader when he recounts how Ellénore called in one of her women friends to help her: 'never hand over the interests of your own heart to anyone else; the heart alone can plead its own case: it alone can measure the depth of the wounds it has suffered; any intermediary becomes a judge' (Ch. VIII, p. 180).

Seriousness and humour

The same pattern of eddying ironies is seen spreading out across the face of the novel when one examines Adolphe's *plaisanterie*, his flippant conversation which serves to hide his real feelings from others. This trait is once again attributed by the narrator to his unsatisfactory relationship with his father. It turns out to be one of the factors which will make him attractive to Ellénore, allowing him to stand out among so many dull-witted men (Ch. II) — a feature, incidentally, so important that Constant altered the passage in the manuscript to give *plaisanterie* prominence at the beginning of a sentence (see *Adolphe*, pp. 122 and 251); it is his *plaisanteries perpétuelles* (the phrase from Ch. I is repeated in the plural in Ch. VI, p. 161) which anaesthetise him in moments of despondency during their liaison, and are also a means by

which he indicates to the Baron de T*** that he is tired of
Ellénore (p. 189). When, at the end of Chapter IX, Adolphe's
witty remarks at her expense are reported back to Ellénore
(p. 192) and she confronts him with his intention of leaving
her, he denies it; with the result that when he writes his fateful
letter to the Baron, Ellénore has once again been lulled into
believing that their lives are 'indissolubly united'. Thus
Adolphe's sense of humour is responsible for his early social
alienation; it is the spark which kindles Ellénore's interest;
and finally, by a line of cause and effect, it is one of the
elements leading to her eventual illness and death, and his
own misery. And was it not after all, by a further irony,
Adolphe taking his father's cynical joke about women
seriously, that led to the affair in the first place?

It might seem odd that the narrator of a story which for
Lord Byron left 'an unpleasant impression' and which many
readers have found unbearably bleak should declare that he
'still' has great difficulty in overcoming his inability to 'con-
verse seriously' (Ch. I, p. 111). Yet critics have tended to pass
over the remark in silence, stressing the other and more immediately accessible part of the sentence, 'hence a certain lack
of spontaneity' or 'a certain inability to let myself go'
(Penguin translation). But it is, I think, worth dwelling for a
moment on Adolphe's acknowledgement of finding it hard to
talk seriously, either at the time the events took place or now
as he writes. I alluded above to elements of dark wit in the
story: Albertine de Staël wrote to Constant when the novel
appeared in 1816 that everyone at Coppet found it 'très
spirituel', 'very witty', a reaction strangely at odds with some
modern accounts of it. Yet there *is* much in *Adolphe*,
especially in the earlier chapters, which is situated on that
borderline – perhaps too seldom recognised or explored –
between what makes us smile and what saddens us. The
tragicomedy of the seduction of Ellénore would fall into
this category, but there are other moments where it is surely
intended that we respond to the fine sense of irony the
narrator displays – and the evident delight in the paradoxical
that shines through despite the painfulness of the experiences

he recounts − with the wry smile which is provoked by the deep recognition of a truth.

Within the space of two pages in Chapter IV there are examples of two such moments: Ellénore informs Adolphe that the Comte de P*** has told her not to receive any more visits from Adolphe and adds that she has no intention of obeying 'this tyrannical order' − a phrase worthy of the most purblind of Molière's characters, so revealing is it both of her lack of awareness of her own despotic attachment to her new lover and of her inability to consider the feelings of her former protector. Then in the course of the same interview she tells Adolphe, who has been eagerly looking forward to being recalled to his father's house so that he can be away from her, that she has decided to leave the Count and her children in order to be entirely his. There is undoubtedly something sad in these two moments, but at the same time something grimly and profoundly comic: in Ellénore being apparently unaware of her own tyranny towards the man she is addressing, and in Adolphe himself, who believes that things are shortly to get much better and who learns to his dismay that they are certain to get far worse. It is surely one of Constant's greatest achievements to maintain through so much of the story a clear eye alert to the often surprisingly incongruous nature of experience, especially when experience proves ultimately to be tragic.

But there is another and no less important aspect of Adolphe's personality that this remark brings out, and a Journal entry gives us a clue to it:

Conversation with Sismondi after dinner. He reproached me for never talking seriously. It is true, but I am too little interested in things or people for them to incline me to anything other than silence or humour. Since I abandoned aiming for a goal I could reach only with the help of others, I cannot be bothered to convince people. But I can take the trouble to amuse myself and forget my sorrows, and since I am always successful with my jokes, I make use of them. The best quality which Heaven gave me is that of being able to find amusement in myself.   (*Œuvres*, p. 370)

Adolphe is not Benjamin Constant, but in this passage, written on 10 September 1804, that is, only two years before

Constant began the novel which would turn into *Adolphe*, there is a revealing parallel. For another dimension of Adolphe's character to which it directs us is one which an attentive reading of the novel confirms: an ability to stand apart from himself, to smile at himself, to observe his own reactions – a reflection, no doubt, of what critics have called *le dédoublement constantien*; but also an ability to play a role, to act, to assume voices and tones which the reader knows do not fit him or which express only a part of his personality.

An example of Adolphe acting out a scene of his own devising occurs in Chapter VI. He has decided to free himself of Ellénore in order to pursue a career, and goes to see her thinking himself immovable in his resolve to make her accept the Comte de P***'s offer to her. His language is that of the worldly wise *roué* who is trying to rid himself of a mistress he has grown tired of: it calls to mind Valmont's letter of farewell to Mme de Tourvel in *Les Liaisons dangereuses*:

My dear, I said to her, one struggles for a while against one's destiny, but in the end one always gives in. The laws of society are stronger than the will of individuals; even the most imperious feelings are broken by the fatal power of circumstances. One persists in vain in consulting only one's heart; sooner or later one has to listen to the voice of reason. I can no longer keep you in a situation as unfitting for you as it is for me. I cannot do it, either for your sake or my own.   (p. 163)

The actor-scriptwriter Adolphe fully intends to convince Ellénore that everything is over between them. But, despite his air of glib self-confidence, he cannot look Ellénore in the eye – the law of *timidité* has begun to operate. He feels his resolve weakening; he reassures her he will always be her friend and will treasure the memory of their two years together (stock items in the seducer's armoury); and finally he blurts out the hurtful truth in all its rawness and with a desperate honesty that has visibly left behind all pretence:

But love – that rapturous flight of feeling, that heady sensation it is impossible to overcome, that forgetfulness of all other interests or duties – Ellénore, I no longer feel it.

We are told how Adolphe loses control of his lines in

Ellénore's presence and tries to prevent her gaze from meeting his. Ironically it is Ellénore's hysteria following upon these brutal but honest words of leave-taking that compels him to pretend in earnest, to tell her that he has deliberately deceived her in order to allow her to be free in her choice between himself and the Count. But what Adolphe has said earlier, though partly false, has in fact been closer to the truth of his wishes than what he is now forced to say. The element of play-acting in Adolphe's behaviour – sometimes ham but successful, on other occasions, as here, unsustainable in the presence of a watchful interlocutor even though, despite badly written lines, he means what he says – calls to mind John Wilde's description of the 'endless mazes' of his friend's character, that Constant who outdid 'even Proteus himself'. The actor Adolphe and his performance are at all times judged by an unsparing critic, the inner observer mentioned in Chapter II, p. 123 ('cette portion de nous, qui est, pour ainsi dire, spectatrice de l'autre', 'that part of us which is, as it were, a spectator watching the rest of us'), a critic who may intervene, as in this instance, while Adolphe is on the stage or may wait till he is leaving it, as when Adolphe nobly defends Ellénore against the Baron de T***'s disparagements in Chapter VII:

I left when I had spoken thus: but who can explain to me that changeableness in my character which made the feelings I expressed die within me even before I had finished uttering them?   (p. 172)

La contrainte

From the years spent with his father Adolphe learns to be an actor, to pretend; he learns to rely on his own inner resources. Consonant with these traits is the growth within him of an overwhelming desire to be independent of other people. The central ironic paradox of the novel is that Adolphe experiences only the *absence* of such freedom throughout most of it. What he feels is only *contrainte*, constraints put on his words and actions, pressures imposed on him by others. No sooner has he won Ellénore's heart than he is complaining to

her about the severe restrictions within which he is now obliged to live (Ch. IV, p. 145), though only a short while before
he had felt the presence of other men at the Comte de P***'s
house as a *contrainte* which prevented him from being alone
with her and had resented it: 'Je ne tardai pas à m'irriter de
tant de contrainte', 'I soon lost patience with so many
restraints' (i.e. on his freedom of action) (Ch. III, p. 132). In
Chapter IV, drawing together the two opposing features of
his existence, he exclaims: 'Encore six mois de gêne et de contrainte! . . . je vis ici sans utilité, sans indépendance, n'ayant
pas un instant de libre, ne pouvant respirer une heure en paix'
(p. 144), 'Still another six months of awkwardness and constraint left! . . . I live here without any purpose to my
existence and without any independence. Not for a second of
my life am I free, nor can I have an hour to myself in which
to breathe in peace.' In Chapter V Adolphe is briefly given a
taste of the 'vie indépendante et tranquille' (p.154), the quiet
and independent life his separation from Ellénore has
brought back to him: he takes positive pleasure in the indifference of others, such a contrast to Ellénore's suffocating
passion for him. (How that indifference of other people will
weigh upon him at the end of the story!) When Adolphe is
once again under Ellénore's domination, his father – so
often the *alter ego* who, like the Baron, gives voice to painful truths which Adolphe himself endeavours to repress –
reminds him in a letter of the principal paradox of his
existence:

I can only feel sorry for the fact that, with your spirit of
independence, you always do what you do not want to do.
(Ch. VII, p. 169)

He ends with a bitter allusion to 'that independence you have
always known how to defend against your father'. It is the
Baron's 'chance' remarks to Adolphe that set him imagining
an ideal companion, a woman who would allow him the
indépendance he misses (Ch. VII, p. 174). Thus we can once
again trace the ironic arabesque of an idea as it runs through
the course of the novel: from *contrainte* with his father –

awkwardness, being constrained to remain silent about his thoughts — comes an impatience with all restrictions, all limits on his freedom; this leads Adolphe to plan the seduction of Ellénore, for reasons we shall examine presently but in part at least as a gesture of self-assertion; thence we come to the misery of his *contrainte habituelle* (Ch. VI, p. 168) during his liaison with Ellénore and at length to the Baron's proffered mirage of happiness and fulfilment without her; and finally to Adolphe's freedom and utter desolation at the close of the story.

It will be clear by now, I hope, that there is far more to the opening paragraphs of the novel than a mere listing of the ways in which Adolphe was affected by his father's treatment of him during his early years. Attitudes, situations and responses described here reproduce themselves in different guises throughout the story and govern its development. So delicate are some of these later variations — in the form of allusions, echoes, identities and contrasts — that it may require several readings of the novel to catch them all. When, for example, Ellénore foresees Adolphe writing her 'des lettres raisonnables' (Ch. VI, p. 165), letters full of good sense which will break her heart, we are surely meant to remember Adolphe's father sending him letters full of 'conseils raisonnables', reasonable advice, about which we are told in the first chapter. In each case Ellénore and the young Adolphe would be hoping to hear something other than cold reason: a fundamentally important analogy between two crucial and troubled relationships is thus re-established discreetly in the reader's mind. A second example of the intricate pattern of variations in *Adolphe* occurs when Ellénore's father comes back into the story, shortly before the end of Chapter VI. At this vital moment in the plot, talk of Ellénore's father reminds Adolphe that he has a duty towards his own father who is still alive. (Ironically his father's friend and agent, the Baron de T*** is on the point of making *his* fateful appearance in the story.) In the following chapter, during his 'night walk', Adolphe visualises his father's joy if he were to find a more suitable partner than Ellénore, one whom his father could accept as a daughter-in-law. This confirms the reader's suspicion that there has been a resurgence of filial piety in Adolphe, a feature of his character carefully delineated in Chapter I, 'I was very aware of [my father's] overwhelming right to my gratitude and respect' (p. 110). One final example will illustrate how dense with allusion and analogy *Adolphe* becomes. There are moments in the paragraph, 'The first year of our stay at Caden . . .', in Chapter VI which seem to point directly back to the initial emotional impasse between father and son. Adolphe and Ellénore criticise each other and then fall back into silence: within a couple of pages of this the narrator takes care to remind us that in his letters to him his father 'never approached any question directly' (Ch. VII, first paragraph). Adolphe and Ellénore miss the right psychological moment to be reconciled: the sentence used to sum up their situation would be an equally fitting description of Adolphe and his father as portrayed in the first chapter of the novel, 'Nos cœurs défiants et blessés ne se rencontraient plus' (p. 166), 'our wounded and distrustful hearts no longer met.' (In fact several sentences which Constant omitted from the final version of *Adolphe* at this point make the parallel yet more explicit, 'We avoided speaking to each other about what we had on our minds. When we were obliged to speak, our discussions were bitter. Ellénore found me hard. I found her unfair. But our arguments did not go on for long' (*Adolphe*, p. 256, list of variants). One can speculate on why these sentences, which seem to echo closely the third and fourth paragraphs of Chapter I, were not included in the final version of the novel. It may be that the facts contained in them were judged by Constant to be implicit in the preceding sentences and that the analogy was sufficiently established there to require no further underlining.)

The sight of suffering

Because of the character traits which the narrator outlines Adolphe feels at his ease only when he is alone − a situation he will achieve to his cost by the end of the story. (The reader is already half-aware of this last fact from the 'Publisher's Note', where Adolphe was glimpsed walking in the evening, always on his own, indeed 'fleeing to deliberate in peace'.) Is it weakness or an extraordinary receptiveness to, and sympathy for the views and feelings of others that makes Adolphe unable to bear anyone near him when he has to choose between two courses of action? This is one of many questions which the novel raises and on which the grounds for judgement are left infinitely complex. A key scene in which Adolphe's reaction to the sight of another person plays a decisive role in the plot is the one we examined earlier, where Adolphe in Chapter VI briefly adopts the role of a seducer who has tired of his mistress. It is seeing Ellénore's pitiful state that induces Adolphe to lie to her — generously, but with an ultimately fatal result. The inner logic of his character in this detail as in others crucially determines the course of events. From the onset of his disenchantment with Ellénore he knows in his heart that, though he may declaim against women's tyrannical power over men, he is unable to ignore a single tear she may shed, cannot hold out against her silent sadness and is 'pursued when away from her by the image of the suffering he [has] caused' (Ch. V, p. 152). In Chapter IV Adolphe's reaction to an expression of suffering has already made him capitulate at a critical moment when he was arguing with Ellénore about prolonging his stay with her by six months:

I tried to oppose her point of view; but she wept so bitterly and was trembling so much, her face bore the marks of such intense suffering that I could not go on. (p. 143)

His father consents to the arrangement; Adolphe stays on with Ellénore long enough for the duel to take place in which he defends her honour; and their relationship becomes closer and deeper, to such an extent that the narrator makes several memorable observations on the unthinkableness of making the break with her when the moment of separation finally arrives, this in the passage which begins 'Il y a dans les liaisons qui se prolongent quelque chose de si profond!'

(Ch. V, pp. 153–4), 'In relationships which go on for a long time there is something so deep!' And, driving home the point about the sight of another person's emotion and distress, the narrator says that if Ellénore had begged him to stay, 'her tears would not have been disobeyed' (p. 153). Adolphe's 'night walk' in Chapter VII is prompted by his inability to face Ellénore after having defended her before the Baron: 'Il me tardait de me trouver seul' (p. 172), 'I longed to be alone'; his anxiety about her after his walk is cut short when he learns that she has been looking for him − 'I was annoyed to see myself subjected by Ellénore to an irksome surveillance' (p. 178) − yet actually seeing her relief touches him; as the narrator deftly puts it, 'Je fus ému de son émotion', 'I was moved by her being so moved.' At the end of Chapter VIII the mere sight of Ellénore in her distress is enough to check his anger; this time, however, as the novel moves towards its climax, her tears (likened, in an unusual and powerful image which recollection of the impossible predicament appears to call forth, to burning lava falling drop by drop on Adolphe's heart), though they may draw cries of anguish from him, are unable to make him deny the truth of the harsh things he has just told Ellénore. A new and critical stage has been reached in the story and the reader shares Ellénore's premonition that sooner or later a decisive outcome will result from this change in Adolphe. Thus from one important thread of personality Constant weaves a pattern that both echoes and contrasts with the initial delineation of Adolphe's character, and in ways which shape the course of events.

Egoism and altruism

Perhaps the oddest of the narrator's statements about his younger self is:

Je n'avais point cependant la profondeur d'égoïsme qu'un tel caractère paraît annoncer: tout en ne m'intéressant qu'à moi, je m'intéressais faiblement à moi-même.   (Ch. I, p. 111)

(I had not, however, that depth of egoism which such a character might seem to suggest: while being interested only in myself, my actual concern with myself was only weak.)

This declaration has been variously glossed by commentators: what appears to be meant is that Adolphe's self-awareness does not make him self-seeking — once again a detail of character that has a profound bearing on the narrative to come. In it lies an explanation of his future predicament. For if he were truly concerned only with seeking his own advantage — as the seducer he at first mistakenly casts himself as would be — he could steel himself to leave Ellénore early on. But in fact he is a man who reflects constantly on the inner world of his thoughts and fluctuating emotions and is hence keenly alert to other people's. The poignant irony of the novel is the degree to which Adolphe's altruism in not immediately making the break with Ellénore prolongs her agony, with the result that when the Baron finally succeeds in arousing that part of Adolphe which is concerned with his own betterment the shock to her proves fatal.

'Un besoin de sensibilité'

That tragic outcome is in a sense foretold in the statement about Adolphe's 'besoin de sensibilité' (Ch. I, p. 111), that is, his need for emotional experience and stimulus — a need 'of which [he] was unaware and which, finding no satisfaction anywhere, removed [him] by turn from everything that at first had aroused [his] curiosity'. For when the initial heady excitement of his affair with Ellénore has worn off — an affair inspired by the vague sense that there was something missing in his life — Adolphe is unable to move on to a new source of stimulus. His deep need is frustrated and he becomes unhappy and restless. On his 'night walk' he finds temporary relief in imagining an ideal companion (a recurrent theme in Constant's Journals), a wife to whom he could show his *sensibilité*, his feelings of tenderness, in an unforced way (Ch. VII, p. 174). Such a possibility is entirely lacking in his relationship with Ellénore. (Interestingly it is here that Adolphe now perceives his need to *show* tenderness to someone rather than passively to absorb love.) During the moment of false calm at the beginning of Chapter X Ellénore

tries once again to force Adolphe into a display of tender
emotion: he has sent his letter to the Baron de T*** and, sens-
ing that he will soon be free of Ellénore, Adolphe is able to
show her 'a more affectionate and sensitive disposition' (Ch.
X, p. 194). This irony which is so cruel for the unsuspecting
Ellénore is matched by that which awaits Adolphe. For feeling has in fact been intensifying in him over the course of
their four years together and, though passion may long since
have evaporated, Adolphe tragically underestimates the
importance to him both of the tenderness, affection and concern which he has for Ellénore, and of Ellénore's passionate
attachment to him. The man we see in the 'Publisher's Note'
– indifferent to everything around him, whether ruins,
monuments or people, indifferent even to the continuance of
his own life, and absorbed by an as yet unexplained grief –
is the Adolphe who has discovered that he has sacrificed
irretrievably the greatest source of emotional fulfilment in his
life. He has sacrificed it in the pursuit of what is now to him
a worthless chimera. Though unsatisfactory and fraught with
irritations, Adolphe's relationship with Ellénore nonetheless
met his deep need to give and inspire emotion. The broken
man who walks alone in the evening (perhaps an ironic
anticipation/echo of the walk in Chapter VII when he
envisages the bliss of being without Ellénore?) is able to read
only in a desultory way, and never travels 'par curiosité', out
of curiosity – an ironic commentary, surely, on the sentence
in Chapter I about Adolphe's rapid loss of interest in those
things which excite his *curiosité*, a loss which results from his
continual need for some new and all-absorbing emotional
experience.

The idea of death

There is perhaps a deep connection between three aspects of
Adolphe's character in particular: first, his tendency not to
consult his own self-interest; second, his need for an outlet
for his emotions, a need undercut by a tendency to short-lived
excitement followed by a relapse into indifference; and third,

the final feature of Adolphe's personality mentioned in the crucial opening pages of the novel — his being so much possessed by the idea of death that as a young man he was filled with uncertainty about the future and with fatalistic apathy towards all human undertakings. We learn that paradoxically this feeling has diminished only as Adolphe has grown older and has drawn inevitably closer to the grave. What links these aspects of Adolphe's personality is perhaps something which Constant may have intuited from his own personal experience, namely the long-term effect on a child of being deprived of sufficient parental love. In the eyes of modern psychologists Adolphe's failure to make a deep and secure bond with the only parent mentioned in the story, his father, could lead to a deep-seated uncertainty about his own worth — a discontent that might give rise to suicidal thoughts — and to a more general morbid obsession with death. This might also produce a tendency to melancholia and recurrent loss of interest in what happens to him. At the end of the story — which we read, of course, at the beginning of the novel in the 'Publisher's Note' — we are told of Adolphe's displeasure at being cured by the village surgeon, a revelation which establishes a certain mood for what is to come. Adolphe also makes what is perhaps a vague threat of suicide to Ellénore ('I must see you if I am to live', Ch. III, p. 131). However it is the less dramatic but debilitating features of this tendency that come into play in the novel and which at critical moments sap Adolphe's will to act.

That Constant himself was a prey to suicidal thoughts as a young man emerges from his letters to Mme de Charrière — though how seriously we ought to take him it is not easy to judge, given the frequently comic tone of the correspondence. But a more general obsession with death was a permanent feature of Constant's personality. Edouard Laboulaye, gathering together in 1861 the memories of those who had known him, quotes J.-J. Coulmann, the close friend of Constant's later years, to the effect that the thought of death remained one of Constant's most besetting concerns. Despite one's suspicion that there may be some degree of reading

Constant back into *Adolphe*, the statement that the novelist 'knew by heart the best verses on death by English, German, Italian and French poets, languages equally familiar to him' does seem to have the ring of an authentic memory. The *Journaux intimes* provide ample corroboration of the anguished uncertainty about how long his life would last which haunted Constant, as in these lines written a few months before he began *Adolphe*:

An impression which life has made upon me and which never leaves me is a kind of terror at the thought of Fate. I never draw a line in my diary to end the day, and I never write tomorrow's date, without a feeling of anxiety about what that unknown tomorrow may bring.
(*Œuvres*, p. 449, entry for 19 January 1805)

In his edition of *Adolphe*, Paul Delbouille quotes from a letter Constant wrote to his aunt Mme de Nassau on 1 February 1796, in which he draws from his preoccupation with mortality a consequence that closely parallels Adolphe's experience: that it is not a fear of death that grows out of the knowledge that one day he will die, so much as a feeling of *detachment from life* which his reason only reinforces (p. 220, note 5). (In all probability Constant's lifelong passion for the risks of gambling for high stakes – with the excitement mingled with terror at the turn of a card which it generated in him – was in some way linked to this more profound sense of uncertainty.) In these respects as in others the compelling coherence and plausibility of Adolphe's behaviour suggest that it was the fruit of a great deal of self-scrutiny on his creator's part.

The theme of death provides a *basso continuo* to the account of Adolphe's experiences. The peculiar power of the idea of death over him is attributed to the unnamed elderly woman, both in consequence of his endless conversations with her in which death figured so prominently, and also of the actual example of her death at which he was present and which he could never afterwards forget. Each of the strands of character which the narrator singles out as deriving from this formative experience – his uncertainty about his destiny, his pensiveness, his taste for poets who dwell on the brevity of life, his feeling that no goal is worth the effort required to achieve it – emerges later during Adolphe's 'night walk' in Chapter VII. They constitute some of the many carefully placed clinching rhymes of situation or attitude that are prepared for in the novel's opening chapter.

The 'night walk' is a *tour de force*, mapping the wanderings of Adolphe's mind as he slips into exactly the kind of 'rêverie vague' alluded to in Chapter I. Turning away from the memory of his painful encounter with the Baron, whose words are seen to echo in his mind (with a cleverly convincing slight degree of distortion so characteristic of memory, p. 173), Adolphe drifts into more distant recollections inspired by the knowledge that Ellénore is the obstacle between himself and success. Anger and frustration sweep over him as he remembers how others far less promising than he have left him far behind on the road to fortune; his imagination begins to work on what might have been – what could yet be – were it not for Ellénore; she becomes a malign ghost condemning him to oblivion; yet despite his rage he knows he cannot bring himself to hurt her. The fantasy of the ideal wife he might marry and the vision of his father's consequent happiness lead Adolphe to muse on the injustice, as he sees it, of Ellénore's wounding reproaches, and he weeps with longing and self-pity when he thinks what he could be to a woman more socially acceptable than Ellénore. His association with a woman who is a social pariah has cut him off forever from the people and places of his childhood, the mental image of which returns to him with a clarity that leaves him shaken. His as yet imaginary woman companion would fit into that cherished world, would help him, and would take him back to a time before the moment when his early promise was blighted. She would give him a second chance. (On 14 February 1805 Constant had written in his Journal: 'Oh for the happiness of a pure marriage in which pleasure is not tainted with disgust, where duty goes hand in hand with enjoyment, where the woman in whose arms you have been lying becomes the friend, the companion of your lifetime, sharing your thoughts and interests!', *Œuvres*, p. 467.) The inward drift continues deeper and deeper,

mingling past, present and ideal future so that the daydream
becomes almost dream. Then Adolphe's attention is harshly
refocused on the outside world: he catches sight of Ellénore's
château. Darkness falling across the countryside prompts a
further reverie, one which seems to contain a memory of the
opening lines of Gray's *Elegy* ('And leaves the World to
Darkness and to me. / Now fades the glimmering Landscape
on the sight, / And all the Air a solemn Stillness holds') –
perhaps one of the English poems Adolphe read with
Ellénore, just as it seems Mme de Charrière and Constant
may have read it together (she quotes from it in a letter to him
of 29 July 1794, *O.C.*, IV, p. 513). Adolphe realises how far
his personal horizons have narrowed through a relationship
that has bruised and humiliated him. But this resurgence of
fretful irritation is calmed by the sight of a light in a cottage
window: the thought that perhaps some poor soul there is
struggling against death allows the narrator to recapitulate in
words similar to those of Chapter I his astonishment that men
should be able to shut out of their minds the inevitability of
death (earlier, 'terme de tout', the end of everything (p. 112),
here 'terme assuré', an end of which we can be certain
(p. 177)). And the conclusion is one of resignation: since life
is short, why should he make another person – Ellénore –
unhappy simply to recapture a few lost years?

> Oh let me abandon these vain exertions: let me enjoy watching time
> pass and my days hurrying by one after the other; let me remain un-
> moved, the detached spectator of an existence that is already half
> spent!   (Ch. VII, p. 177)

Adolphe's irritation vanishes, and with it all bitterness
towards Ellénore. As so minutely anticipated in Chapter I, a
fatalistic calm descends on Adolphe, one induced by the
culminating meditation on death – and the most serious stirring yet of revolt against what he at one point calls his 'long
and shameful degradation' fails to go any further. Adolphe's
'imagination rebelle', his rebellious imagination (Ch. X,
p. 197), after calling forth the ethereal form of the perfect
wife and evoking scenes that fed his sense of discontent and
isolation, now finally summons up an image that puts an end

to any impulse to effect a change in his situation. By a tragic irony the thought of death delays a decision to leave Ellénore which might in the long run have spared her life.

Religion and scepticism

It is of course in that final episode of the novel, the death of Ellénore, that Adolphe's feelings about mortality surface again and take on a new dimension. In her last hours Ellénore turns to her religion — as she is Polish it is reasonable to assume that she is a Roman Catholic — and is visited by a priest. Adolphe is an outsider to the proceedings, doubly so since he remains in the background while the priest and others say prayers and he appears to be of a different religious denomination. From his vantage point in the corner of Ellénore's bedroom he observes the different reactions of those gathered around the dying woman, the terror it inspires in some, others whose minds are clearly not on the proceedings, but most especially the effect of habit on religious rituals which dulls the sense of their awesomeness. Here the narrator brings together a theme introduced late in Chapter I, that of the tendency to slip into conventional ways of thought which prevent a lively apprehension of reality, and that of people's ability to ignore the fact that one day they will die. As the narrator says, those present repeat the words of the ritual 'as if they themselves were not going to die one day'. There is here, however, a significant change in Adolphe's attitude: gone is the earlier disdain for that which is commonly believed:

But I was certainly not inclined to pour scorn on these practices. Is there one of them which man in his ignorance would dare to pronounce as useless . . . I am not surprised that man needs a religion, but rather that he thinks himself strong enough, sufficiently insulated from unhappiness, to dare to reject any of them.

(Ch. X, p. 202)

We can measure the distance he has travelled between the death of the elderly lady in Chapter I and the imminent death of Ellénore: the aggressive scepticism he developed in the company of the older woman has given way to a sympathetic understanding of those who need the comfort and consolation of religious ritual. Adolphe's development mirrors that of Constant himself: from Enlightenment incredulity Constant had progressed, by way of a fascination with the religions of antiquity, to a point where he could tell his friend Claude Hochet in a letter dated 11 October 1811, echoing Pascal, that 'a little knowledge leads to atheism, and more knowledge to religion' (quoted by Gustave Rudler, *La Jeunesse de Benjamin Constant*, Paris, 1909, p. 178). It is important to be clear: Adolphe like his creator Constant does not himself acquire positive beliefs, but reaches a point where the religious instinct is no longer scorned. Religion is not a consolation that Adolphe himself turns to: his suffering at the loss of Ellénore seems unmitigated by any belief in an after-life.

A parallel: *René*

Adolphe's melancholia and often downcast air are part of his charm for Ellénore (Ch. II, p. 122). In fact these are one of the subtly drawn parallels between their characters: as early as in Chapter IV (p. 142) she speaks about dying in Adolphe's arms. And of course the Baron de T*** in his glib generalisations about women ignores the *uniqueness* of Ellénore: other women may protest that they will die if they are abandoned by their lover, and not mean it; Ellénore tells Adolphe how she has genuinely longed for death in her despair and implored Heaven to grant it to her. Her predictions are given tangible form in the letter written at an earlier period than that of her final illness, at a moment in their relationship when she was more bitter and vengeful than during the last days of rediscovered tenderness (Ch. X, p. 205). This melancholy and concern with death in both characters has many literary antecedents – Julie and Saint-Preux in Rousseau's *La Nouvelle Héloïse* (1761) exhibited similar features; Werther read the poetry of Ossian. There is a family resemblance too with William and Caliste in Mme de Charrière's *Caliste*, where the heroine likewise foresees a tragic end for herself.

But the parallels with Chateaubriand's *René* (1802) are of special interest. René, a young man 'timide et contraint' in his father's presence like Adolphe, turns to his sister Amélie for warmth and she conceives an incestuous passion for him. René is the Romantic figure *par excellence* in French literature, and his life story and character are strangely close in some respects to Constant's: his mother dies giving birth to him; there is a family château near a lake in the provinces; it is hinted that, like Adolphe, René is not shown enough love by his father; like Adolphe too his character is a mixture of vitality and melancholy, gregariousness and liking for solitude. The death of his father in his arms makes a lasting impression on René. There are other analogies: the closing comments by Chactas and Father Souël on René's *récit*, the autumn walks which René takes with his sister during which they crush the dead leaves under their feet. But if there is an influence of *René* in *Adolphe*, the way in which Constant improves on Chateaubriand's most famous creation is instructive: in *Adolphe*, as we have seen, the *timidité* and *contrainte* are tied into the story in the firmest way through Adolphe's actions, contributing to the achievement of a complex mesh of circumstances and problems; the style is incisive and unfaltering both in its elegant clarity and scrupulous economy, unlike the vague, exclamatory and rhapsodic manner of Chateaubriand; the winter walk which Adolphe and Ellénore take at the end of the novel is specially memorable because it is frozen grass that they walk on in the weak sunshine, emblematic of Ellénore's brief recovery soon to be followed by her death.

The conventions of society

The theme of death is amplified through the account in Chapter I of Adolphe's relationship with the elderly lady whose career, so bright at the outset because of her great intellectual gifts, comes to nothing because of her refusal to bend to the 'convenances factices, mais nécessaires' (p. 112), the artificial but necessary code of behaviour of society. She sees her youth pass without pleasure, and her hopes disappointed. The reader's sense that there is an undertone of foreboding in this brief evocation of unfulfilled promise is of course borne out by subsequent events: it is a foreshadowing of Adolphe's experiences, taking up the idea of hopes and expectations, *espérances*, from the first lines of the novel, hopes which are thwarted for similar reasons. But there is a vital difference between Adolphe and the woman: he lacks her defiant strength of character, for it is by complying with society's wishes as expressed through the Baron de T*** that he is responsible for his final misery. The fate of the 'femme âgée' is also ominous in the light of what we shortly learn about Ellénore: if Adolphe lacks the elderly woman's willpower, Ellénore lacks her powerful intellect that allows her to judge society against an independent standard.

This brings us to the last important function of the opening chapter of *Adolphe*, that of introducing the theme of original as against received or orthodox thought. When he arrives in the small German town of D*** the traits of Adolphe's character, so carefully documented as we have seen, now come swiftly into play. Timidity makes him unable to profit fully from the welcome extended to him; his preference for solitude and his appearance of cool detachment are soon interpreted as the marks of a proud or ill-natured young man, and he becomes the object of criticism. But his position is made much worse by his tendency to be carried away on those occasions when he does speak in company and to make caustic observations at the expense of those around him. Here the final piece in the mosaic of Adolphe's character is fitted into place, his extreme aversion for conventional ideas and for all dogmatic assertions, whether on social behaviour, morality or religion. This was an antipathy reinforced by many conversations with his older woman friend. It was not, as the narrator says, so much the actual content of people's beliefs that irritated him as the complacent and doctrinaire way in which they were held, the 'ponderous and immovable conviction' that became attached to them. As we have seen, by the end of the novel Adolphe, though remaining sceptical in his attitudes, does acquire a tolerant sympathy at least as far as religious beliefs are concerned. Indeed what gives *Adolphe* its tonic intellectual power are the observations of the narrator (who is an older Adolphe reliving through the narrative his relationship with Ellénore), his vigilance vis-à-vis conventional ways of thinking, and his acute sense of the labyrinthine complexity of human experience. The last pages of Chapter I are given over to the way in which such a mind reacts to the cramped norms and petrified clichés of society and becomes alienated from it. But the account of this process is carefully balanced, as throughout the novel, by the narrator's awareness – which comes only with age and experience – of the immense power of the social group whose rules and codes, at times arbitrary-seeming, are nonetheless essential to the continued smooth running of society. In a striking paragraph the older Adolphe reflects on the nature of society's influence on the youthful and dissenting individual, and his remarks bear also on the course of his own life:

[Society] weighs so heavily upon us, its insidious influence is so powerful, that within a short while it fashions us to the same mould as everyone else. Afterwards we are only surprised that we could ever have been surprised [i.e. about the ways of society], and we are perfectly at ease in our new incarnation, just as in a crowded theatre one is at length able to breathe freely whereas on entering one had difficulty in finding one's breath.   (Ch. I, p. 115)

And the narrator makes a distinction between himself and the rare, exceptional individual who is able to stand apart from society in silent scorn: Adolphe's witticisms and mockery are not the mark of a strong-minded and steadfast dissident, and in that lies the germ of his ultimate downfall. In his attempts to find some judicious compromise between the different demands that will be made upon him – society's pressure on him to terminate an irregular relationship, his own desire to be free of a woman he feels he no longer loves and to exercise his talents within society, Ellénore's desperate fear of being abandoned – Adolphe is like the rest of humanity: he is Everyman, and his predicament takes on a general significance.

Adolphe and Ellénore

There is no doubt a central paradox hidden in Adolphe's behaviour. At the end of his life Constant returned to a theme which became the keynote of his political campaigning as well as of so much of his writing. In the second of two articles entitled *Réflexions sur la tragédie* ('Reflections on Tragedy') which appeared in the *Revue de Paris* in 1829 he praised a play by the German dramatist Ludwig Robert, *Die Macht der Verhältnisse*, 'The Force of Circumstance' − a title which, incidentally, Constant preferred to translate as 'la force des préjugés', 'the power of [social] prejudices'. Constant stressed that aspect of the play which concerns the prejudices of polite society and those who are the victims of those prejudices or class distinctions:

The principal character in Monsieur Robert's tragedy is, then, a man oppressed by social prejudices and institutions. The dramatist has had the happy notion of at the same time presenting him as a conscientious defender of those same institutions and prejudices − an ingenious way of showing how inexorable they are in their workings.

(Œuvres, p. 959)

The parallel with the end of *Adolphe* is, on reflection, an unmistakable one: Constant's novel is the paradoxical story of a conspicuously rebellious young man who is at length induced to be reconciled with society − at the price of Ellénore's life, whose existence alone gives his own some meaning and purpose, though he realises this fact too late. Ellénore herself, as we see in Chapter II, is caught on the same knife-edge as Adolphe, though from the outset she is seen supporting − internalising − the social prejudices which oppress her as they oppress the hero in Robert's play. As a part of his strategy of building up the similarities as well as the differences between the two central figures in the reader's mind, Constant sees to it that the narrator characterises Adolphe's behaviour in society as a young man in two sentences which in their balance exactly match those which will shortly be used of Ellénore:

Quelquefois je cherchais à contraindre mon ennui; je me réfugiais dans une taciturnité profonde: on prenait cette taciturnité pour du dédain. D'autres fois, lassé moi-même de mon silence, je me laissais aller à quelques plaisanteries, et mon esprit, mis en mouvement, m'entraînait au-delà de toute mesure.   (Ch. I, p. 113)

(Sometimes I tried to hide my boredom; I took refuge in prolonged silence: my silence was taken for disdain. On other occasions, tired of remaining silent, I fell to making jokes and once my sense of humour was active I became carried away, beyond what was acceptable.)

Ellénore is 'often pensive and taciturn', but sometimes falls to talking endlessly (Ch. II, p. 121). The outward parallels in behaviour are established but, as the reader knows, the reasons for that similarity are quite different. Intellectual boredom is the explanation for Adolphe's taciturn moments: when he speaks it is to give vent to his impatience at the certainties of those around him. With Ellénore, however, her withdrawal into silence and her spells of animated conversation derive from her position as a kept woman which is at odds with both social convention and the requirements of her religion. Irritation with conventionally accepted ideas on the one hand, and on the other a desperate desire to achieve conventional respectability: the mutual attraction on the part of these two social misfits, it is suggested, grows out of a fundamental misapprehension about each other – one which, in the long run, will prove to be a tragic mistake.

Chapter 6

The portrait of Ellénore

Ellénore n'avait qu'un esprit ordinaire; mais ses idées étaient justes, et ses expressions, toujours simples, étaient quelquefois frappantes par la noblesse et l'élévation de ses sentiments. Elle avait beaucoup de préjugés; mais tous ses préjugés étaient en sens inverse de son intérêt. Elle attachait le plus grand prix à la régularité de la conduite, précisément parce que la sienne n'était pas régulière suivant les notions reçues. Elle était très religieuse, parce que la religion condamnait rigoureusement son genre de vie. Elle repoussait sévèrement dans la conversation tout ce qui n'aurait paru à d'autres femmes que des plaisanteries innocentes, parce qu'elle craignait toujours qu'on ne se crût autorisé par son état à lui en adresser de déplacées. Elle aurait désiré ne recevoir chez elle que des hommes du rang le plus élevé et de mœurs irréprochables, parce que les femmes à qui elle frémissait d'être comparée se forment d'ordinaire une société mélangée, et, se résignant à la perte de la considération, ne cherchent dans leurs relations que l'amusement. Ellénore, en un mot, était en lutte constante avec sa destinée. Elle protestait, pour ainsi dire, par chacune de ses actions et de ses paroles, contre la classe dans laquelle elle se trouvait rangée: et comme elle sentait que la réalité était plus forte qu'elle, et que ses efforts ne changeaient rien à sa situation, elle était fort malheureuse. Elle élevait deux enfants qu'elle avait eus du comte de P***, avec une austérité excessive. On eût dit quelquefois qu'une révolte secrète se mêlait à l'attachement plutôt passionné que tendre qu'elle leur montrait, et les lui rendait en quelque sorte importuns. Lorsqu'on lui faisait à bonne intention quelque remarque sur ce que ses enfants grandissaient, sur les talents qu'ils promettaient d'avoir, sur la carrière qu'ils auraient à suivre, on la voyait pâlir de l'idée qu'il faudrait qu'un jour elle leur avouât leur naissance. Mais le moindre danger, une heure d'absence, la ramenait à eux avec une anxiété où l'on démêlait une espèce de remords, et le désir de leur donner par ses caresses le bonheur qu'elle n'y trouvait pas elle-même. Cette opposition entre ses sentiments et la place qu'elle occupait dans le monde avait rendu son humeur fort inégale. Souvent elle était rêveuse et taciturne; quelquefois elle parlait avec impétuosité. Comme elle était tourmentée d'une idée particulière, au milieu de la conversation la plus générale, elle ne restait jamais parfaitement calme. Mais, par cela même, il y avait dans sa manière

quelque chose de fougueux et d'inattendu qui la rendait plus pi-
quante qu'elle n'aurait dû l'être naturellement. La bizarrerie de sa
position suppléait en elle à la nouveauté des idées. On l'examinait
avec intérêt et curiosité comme un bel orage.   (Ch. II, pp. 120–1)

(Ellénore was of only average intelligence, but her ideas were sound
and the words with which she expressed herself, while always plain,
were sometimes striking because of the nobility and loftiness of her
feelings. She had many fixed opinions, but all of them ran counter to
her self-interest. She set great store by regularity of conduct precisely
because her own was not regular when judged by conventional standards. She was very religious because religion severely condemned her
way of life. She banned from polite conversation what to other women
would have appeared merely innocent jests because she was afraid that
knowing of her situation, people might feel at liberty to make her the
object of an indelicate witticism. She would have liked to receive in her
drawing-room only men of the highest rank and of irreproachable
morals because the kind of women with whom she shuddered to think
she might be compared generally find themselves surrounded by a
rather mixed company: resigning themselves to the loss of all respect in
the eyes of society, they look only for amusement in their social relationships. Ellénore was, in short, constantly struggling against her
fate. Her every word and action was, one might say, a protest against
the position to which she found herself relegated. Since she knew that
reality was stronger than she was, and since all her efforts did nothing
to change her situation, she was very unhappy. She had had two
children by the Comte de P*** and brought them up with excessive
strictness. Sometimes one sensed that she was secretly in revolt against
the attachment which she felt for them, an attachment which was more
passionate than tender, and that this made her children somehow
irksome to her. When anyone made a well-intentioned remark on the
fact that they were growing up, on the talents which they seemed likely
to display in the future, or on the career which they ought to pursue,
she would grow pale at the thought that one day she would have to tell
her children of the circumstances of their birth. But if she believed that
they were in the slightest danger or if she was away from them even for
an hour, she would rush to their side filled with an anxiety in which one
felt there was a kind of remorse: it seemed that in her caresses she
wished to give her children the happiness which they did not give her.
The opposition between Ellénore's feelings and the place which she
occupied in society had made her temperament very changeable.
Often she was pensive and silent; sometimes she would talk with great
animation. Tormented by her private thoughts in the midst of the most
general conversation, she was never able to remain perfectly calm. But
it was precisely this which gave Ellénore a certain impulsiveness

and unpredictability, and made her more intriguing than she would otherwise have been. The peculiarity of her situation made up for her lack of original ideas. She was observed with interest and curiosity like a magnificent thunderstorm.)

Constant lived the greater part of his life in the eighteenth century, thirty-three of his sixty-three years, and in taste, sensibility and literary imagination he remained attached to the canons of French Classical writing. The paragraph quoted above, the description of Ellénore, belongs to a literary genre which enjoyed a considerable vogue throughout eighteenth-century Europe, that of the literary portrait, whose origins could be traced to La Bruyère's *Caractères* (1688) or further still to Theophrastus. It was not uncommon among those of an artistic inclination to produce a sketch in words of a friend or indeed of themselves – the 'Character of H. B. Constant' by John Wilde quoted above at the beginning of Chapter 2 is a fine example of this in English. The portrait or extended character-description found a natural place in the relatively new art form of the novel where, placed as here at the beginning of an action, it set a new character firmly in the reader's mind and offered clues to be followed through, expectations to be realised in later scenes. The character portrait endures still in the late twentieth century, being perhaps an irreplaceable weapon in a story-teller's armoury. Like so much else about *Adolphe*, what distinguishes the portrait we see here is the limpidity and terseness of the prose wedded to a curiosity about human behaviour that flinches at no complexity or contradiction, that resolutely sets out to trace thought and action to their origin. As was mentioned before, in its close and exacting contemplation and presentation of psychological reality *Adolphe* bears a strong resemblance to an earlier masterpiece of the French *roman d'analyse*, Madame de Lafayette's *La Princesse de Clèves* (1678), though in its syntax it is far simpler. The psychological investigation which Constant undertakes owes something too to the work of La Rochefoucauld: he is a *moraliste* – as distinct from *moralisateur* – in applying his clear-sighted inquiring intelligence to a search for the hidden motives behind thoughts and actions in order to attain a deeper understanding of human nature, not in order to preach or moralise. As a consequence character is revealed in *Adolphe* not only in its broad visible outlines but in its more secret byways and recesses, necessitating an art which rests on seizing the elusive nuance; on seeing how an excess or a lack of a quality has consequences elsewhere in a personality; on the ability to show how contradictory attributes can co-exist within an individual. Constant's handling of adversative conjunctions here as elsewhere in *Adolphe* is instructive: *mais*, 'but', or *cependant*, 'however', 'yet'. He has a sense of the unfathomably complex life of the mind, where at each second a feeling can shade off abruptly into another, not infrequently its opposite. Indeed this is stated earlier in Chapter II of *Adolphe*: 'Les sentiments de l'homme sont confus et mélangés; ils se composent d'une multitude d'impressions variées qui échappent à l'observation', 'People's emotions are confused and intermingled; they are made up of a multitude of varying impressions which always escape the eye of the observer.'

There is no physical description of Ellénore here or elsewhere in the novel. We are told that she is ten years older than Adolphe, and though she is still beautiful, she is no longer 'de la première jeunesse'. Indeed we can visualise her appearance far less clearly perhaps than that of the characters of *La Princesse de Clèves*. What matter are her position in society, the difference of age between herself and Adolphe, her knowledge that her beauty is beginning to fade. The portrait of her is a *portrait moral*, it presents Ellénore's situation – her predicament – as that of a woman in contradiction with herself. Accordingly, it is cast for the most part in the imperfect tense of description or repeated action appropriate to a personality and a state of mind viewed over a period of time. The material, concrete or physical is brought in only insofar as it has a bearing on Ellénore's attitudes, opinions or emotions – 'she would grow pale'. She is revealed in a series of contrasts, by antitheses and antithetical groups: her intellect is not exceptional but her ideas are sound; the words with which she expresses herself are simple, yet they can sometimes be striking; she has many prejudices, yet all of them run counter to her own self-interest; she sets great store by regularity of conduct − her own, however, is irregular when judged by conventional standards; she is religious *because* religion condemns her way of life as a kept woman, and so on. Under Constant's pen even a simple *parce que*, 'because' takes on the force of an adversative, here by linking the two elements of a paradox, and one remembers the similarly sharp stab of the *parce que* in La Rochefoucauld's *Maximes* (1664) where it is used to explain some subterfuge of the ego of which we were hitherto unconscious, or which we did not wish to see. The balance, the scrupulous sense of proportion in judgement which Constant's sentences exhibit is not merely there in tribute to the French Classical ideal of harmony in prose: it is in the service of the novelist's effort to weigh and discriminate, and to show reasons behind a character's behaviour.

The passage as a whole falls into two parts, the first closing with the sentence 'Ellénore was, in short, constantly struggling against her fate.' The first section of the passage summarises Ellénore's situation and her reaction to it as revealed in her public life. The second goes deeper and speculates on why Ellénore feels and acts as she does with her two children, at length returning to her effect on people in general. There is a circularity about the portrait: it begins and ends on her unremarkable intelligence, the lack of novelty in her ideas made up for in part by puritanical behaviour curious for one in her position. Another unusual feature of the passage, and one recently remarked on by the Swiss narratologist Jean-Luc Seylaz in a highly original article, is that for all the interest in narrative technique in *Adolphe* shown by modern critics it appears to have gone largely unnoticed that the description of Ellénore, crucial as it is to our understanding of the novel, is in fact not given by a *je* ('I') narrator at all but by an unexplained 'one'. The paragraghs which precede and follow it are full of *je*, *moi*, *mon*, *mes* and ultimately of the *nous* of Adolphe and Ellénore, yet here we are presented with an

Ellénore *before Adolphe knew her*, as seen by a disinterested and highly observant spectator, possibly, we assume, an habitué of her drawing room. Although there is no evidence in the manuscript of *Adolphe* that the passage was a late interpolation, we do know that Constant's method of work was often to put aside passsages with which he was pleased and to fit them into his works where he could find a use for them − the well-known paragraph which begins Chapter IV, 'Charme de l'amour, qui pourrait vous peindre!', was added late to the novel, perhaps at proof stage: it is not found in the manuscript and may well have once belonged elsewhere. Be that as it may, the description of Ellénore does have a somewhat special feel to it − Seylaz likens it to a 'morceau obligé' (set piece) − and this is reinforced by the almost unique shift in narrative perspective. (Interestingly, the other exception to the omnipresent I − narrator within the story is the 'Charme de l'amour' interpolation whose *nous* according to Seylaz is that of happy lovers, not of Adolphe and Ellénore, and appears briefly from out of nowhere.) Ellénore's portrait is of course, nonetheless, an indispensable part of the novel. It is not simply a set-piece exercise by an eighteenth-century connoisseur of character: it gives information vital to our understanding of everything that ensues and to the novel's central theme, that of the relationship of men and women in a particular historical society. In it we learn of Ellénore's long struggle for some kind of social rehabilitation and of her love for her children, both of these being things which she is shortly to sacrifice by her affair with Adolphe. The picture of her is built up through verbal oppositions: Ellénore is shown to be the locus of conflict and contradiction. In addition to the oppositions we have already noted, we are told, in connection with her children, that she has brought them up with an 'austérité excessive', *yet* that she only wants their happiness; that they are a perpetual source of embarrassment to her because they are illegitimate, *yet* she is fearful lest anything should happen to them (and perhaps rather possessive); that she appears lacking in tenderness towards them, *despite* a passionate outward display of affection. In company she is at times silent and lost in thought, at other moments liable to break into a torrent of conversation. There is an undercurrent of agitation and worry at work in her at all times: even when engaged in an innocuous general conversation, some thought at the back of her mind – one presumes the haunting obsession with her loss of respectability – will not give her peace. Ellénore is associated with words which recall the idea of discord and conflict: 'lutte' ('struggle'), 'Elle protestait', 'révolte secrète', 'opposition', or more generally with words underlining the febrile, even violent intensity of her feelings, 'expressions . . . frappantes' ('striking expressions'), 'repoussait sévèrement' ('severely rejected'), 'austérité excessive', 'anxiété', 'humeur fort inégale' ('very uneven temperament'), 'impétuosité', 'tourmentée . . . jamais parfaitement calme', 'quelque chose de fougueux et d'inattendu' ('impulsive and unpredictable'), and finally 'bel orage' ('magnificent storm'). She is never at rest because she is at odds with herself and at odds with society: at odds with herself *because* she is at odds with society. We recall the circular form of the passage which begins and closes with the notion of Ellénore's unexceptional mind, the commonplace nature of her thought: she is trapped by her 'esprit ordinaire', an ordinary woman caught in an exceptional situation and unable to rise above society's conventions and shibboleths, accepting its moral code (with all its contradictions) as right while failing to conform to it. Ellénore could hardly be more unlike the Marquise de Merteuil of Laclos' *Les Liaisons dangereuses* (1782), the heroic-satanic rebel against the role imposed on women by society and against the disparity in standards of sexual behaviour expected of men and women. Mme de Merteuil was 'née pour venger mon sexe et maîtriser le vôtre' ('born to avenge my sex and to dominate yours'), as she tells the Vicomte de Valmont in letter 81 of Laclos' novel. Ellénore, however, does not have ideas of her own about right and wrong in such matters, but rather condemns herself for not following the conventional pattern – society's – which she has adopted. 'Les notions reçues', society's standards of morality – disparities and unfairnesses notwithstanding — and her own religious sentiments condemn her to unremitting anxiety: her mode of life proclaims her unwilling rebellion against society's values, and that rebellion is internalised as guilt. At the same time she has made strenuous efforts to redress the balance in society's eyes: her ability to sacrifice herself for the Comte de P***, her loyalty to him during a difficult period of his life, her unstinting struggles on his behalf are well known in the circles in which they both move, and her actions have won Ellénore a little credit. Nevertheless she knows that without the Comte de P*** she would become a pariah, an outcast exposed to the full vehemence of society's contempt. The precariousness of her social station adds to her anxiety. She remains proud, knowing that she is worthy of better consideration than society will ever give her. She lives as if she were a respectable woman, as if she had not permanently forfeited her right to all esteem. And society, as she knows, is unjust in the unequal severity of its treatment of men and women in sexual matters: only women can be deemed to have 'fallen'. Men's aberrations are merely winked at as peccadilloes; they may even be encouraged. (Adolphe's father cynically parodies the indulgent attitude which women are expected to adopt towards men's desire for sexual pleasure.) Ellénore can do nothing to improve her situation: struggle as she may she will get nowhere as long as she continues to lead an 'irregular' life. Her one mistake will not be forgiven.

In an earlier draft of the novel Constant described Ellénore as having had an 'avanture [sic] d'éclat', a relationship of some public notoriety with another man before she met the Comte (Adolphe, p. 251). On the advice of Lady Charlotte Campbell this did not appear in the final printed version of Adolphe: Constant was told that the first affair would destroy all interest in Ellénore (Adolphe, p. 222), and quite apart from the moral offence it would have given to a contemporary audience — a confirmation if any were needed of Adolphe's close reflection of society's attitudes — one can see that the artistic reasons for suppressing the early affair are strong: in the final version nothing is allowed to detract from the poignancy of Ellénore's position. Her portrait reveals that her life has reached an unhappy impasse before Adolphe ever comes on the scene: she exists uneasily in a social limbo on the margins of respectable society. In the one paragraph under consideration the fact that she is a man's mistress is alluded to several times, echoing polite euphemisms: '[sa conduite] n'était pas régulière', 'son genre de vie', 'son état', 'la classe dans laquelle elle se trouvait rangée', 'sa situation', 'la place qu'elle occupait', 'sa position'. The portrayal of Ellénore's plight epitomises the fate of so many in her position in eighteenth- and nineteenth-century Europe. What may be less clear but is important from an artistic viewpoint is that Ellénore has several literary antecedents, one of which at least is of considerable significance.

The theme of the fallen woman and her problematic rehabilitation as a member of respectable society is no doubt one very particular development in Western literature's perennial concern with the sanctity of marriage, a concern which has expressed itself in literature from *Tristan et Iseult* in the Middle Ages to Tolstoy's *Anna Karenina* and beyond, and which has been exhaustively treated by Denis de Rougemont in *L'Amour et l'Occident* (*Passion and Society*). All of eighteenth-century educated Europe had been swept with enthusiasm for Rousseau's *La Nouvelle Héloïse* (1761) and its story of the doomed love affair between Julie d'Etange and Saint-Preux, and of her efforts to put her sinful past behind her after her marriage to M. de Wolmar. Appended to Rousseau's vast novel is the tale of Laure Pisana, sold by her parents when young to a cardinal, a woman who in later life through her love for Lord Bomston is restored to a sense of shame for her earlier conduct: as Rousseau says, in Laure 'la pudeur éteinte était revenue avec l'amour' ('her lost modesty returned to her when she discovered love'). This memory prevents Laure from consummating her love for the Englishman; he for his part begins to feel the pressure of society on him and hesitates between Laure and another woman. The episode finally peters out in indecision. It is indecision too, on the part of the man she loves and whom she hopes to marry, that is the cause of Caliste's unhappiness and ultimately of her death in Mme de Charrière's novel of the same name (1787). Caliste displays a sense of pride in her reconquered virtue strikingly similar to that of Rousseau's Laure. The theme of the 'fallen woman' was touched on in Marceline's celebrated feminist manifesto in Beaumarchais' *Le Mariage de Figaro* (1784), in a biting passage that suggests that there is one law for men and another for women. But *Caliste* and its heroine are of very special significance in view of Mme de Charrière's role in Constant's early emotional and artistic development. The great difference between *Caliste* and *Adolphe* is that in Mme de Charrière's novel Caliste and William do not sexually consummate their relationship.

However, once this is said, one cannot but be struck by the many parallels of character and situation: both Caliste and Ellénore are women with a past, Caliste's irregular liaison with an aristocrat having taken place some time before the story begins, Ellénore's continuing in the present: each dies as a consequence of her relationship with the man she truly loves. William in *Caliste* and Adolphe are inexperienced in love and find that their fathers are hostile to their partners on social grounds. To different degrees this hostility contributes to the delay and prevarication on the part of the irresolute hero on which the plot of each novel turns. Constant knew *Caliste* extremely well, perhaps almost by heart, and refers to it several times with admiration in his letters to Mme de Charrière and in the *Cahier rouge*. It was indeed a desire to emulate his friend's achievement which may have led Constant to collaborate with her on the *Lettres de d'Arsillé fils* in 1787–8, a text whose theme anticipates *Adolphe* to some degree. It is not surprising therefore to find echoes of *Caliste* in *Adolphe*, not least in the portrait of Ellénore. Caliste's fall from virtue was the result of her mother's cynically 'selling' her to Lord L. after Caliste's performance on the London stage in a production of Nicholas Rowe's *The Fair Penitent* – from this she had acquired the name of Rowe's heroine Calista. In Ellénore's case it was her mother's death which left her totally isolated: the narrator states that he never discovered exactly how the liaison with the Comte de P*** began, although the implication is that being alone in the world, far from her father and in straitened circumstances, induced her to look favourably on a man who said he loved her. Educated in every accomplishment at Lord L.'s expense, Caliste lived with her lover and benefactor for some years, his death leaving her with the indelible reputation of having once been a 'kept woman'. Caliste is talented in the arts, and in this she resembles the heroine of *Corinne* (1807) who also undoubtedly owes something to Mme de Charrière's novel which *Corinne*'s author, Mme de Staël, like Constant greatly admired. Despite superficial differences Caliste is torn by the same contradictory feelings as Ellénore, as William's retrospective narrative emphasises:

Dependent on others although she was adored by many, despised by some and yet treated with reverence by others, she had become a prey to a certain sad reserve which was partly the result of pride, partly of fear. If she had been less loving, she might have appeared unsociable and shy.   (*O.C.*, VIII, p. 193)

In Lord L.'s drawing-room, Caliste tells William,

people . . . had grown so used to me that often without noticing it they said the most insulting things in my presence. On many occasions I smiled at Lord L. to indicate that he should let them carry on talking; sometimes I was relieved that they had forgotten what I was, at other times I was flattered that they regarded me as an exception among women of my kind.   (*O.C.*, VIII, p. 193)

Social conversation is a continual source of torment, a problem for which the more assertive Ellénore provides a characteristically extreme solution. We are never told why the Comte de P*** did not marry his mistress; Mme de Charrière makes Lord L.'s explanation of why he will not marry Caliste the occasion for an acerbic footnote. Lord L. tells her that he is financially ruined and that she would gain no money by their legal union. He asks her whether she would be any better off as a penniless widow with a title:

Either I am wrong about society, or the woman who has gained nothing from being my companion except the pleasure of making the man who loved her the happiest of mortals, will be more respected

than would the woman to whom I left a surname and a title.
(*O.C.*, VIII, p. 194)

The footnote laconically observes: 'He was wrong about society and his reasoning was faulty.' Mme de Charrière's life had made her aware at every moment of a woman's vulnerability if she dared to go against conventional taboos.

Our conclusion so far, then, is that Ellénore's portrait encapsulates a number of social and moral dilemmas which had been the subject of other novels, most notably of *Caliste*, and that, while Constant's own observation of life had of course made him perfectly aware of the truth of what he is presenting in the description of Ellénore, the example of Mme de Charrière's work may well have helped him in the shaping of his portrayal.

But the description of Ellénore is bound by multiple roots and filaments to the story of Adolphe's relationship with her, which is the central concern of the novel. The passage's importance cannot be separated from its place in the flow of a narrative full of the interplay of echo and allusion, every part organically dependent for its full meaning on what precedes and follows it. And what comes immediately after the 'portrait' in the rest of Chapter II and in Chapter III is Adolphe's consuming desire to conquer Ellénore – out of vanity, boredom and the wish for intense emotional experience – and then the exquisite, overwhelming but short-lived experience of being head over heels in love with her. In the description of Ellénore and in the paragraphs which come before and after, we see both the reality of Ellénore and the magical illusion that Adolphe's mind weaves around her. Her struggle to express herself in a foreign language lends her ideas an originality the older narrator now knows they did not possess, and the implication is discreetly established in the reader's mind that the younger Adolphe found in her a shadowy and appealing reminder of his formative relationship five years before with an older and highly intellectual woman. (Ellénore's much-discussed Polish nationality is, surely, entirely appropriate: her pride, her sense of humiliation and dispossession are a parallel to her nation's struggle to regain its freedom and independence at the end of the eighteenth century, a struggle which never failed to strike a deep chord in Constant as his correspondence shows, though he realistically anticipated the inevitable defeat of every rebellion.) But the misapprehensions are not all on Adolphe's part: Ellénore is astonished and delighted by this restless, now sardonic, now melancholy exception in a world of dull men with business to attend to and regular occupations. Adolphe is an unstable mix of qualities, however, and likely to bring less relief to her perpetual agitation than the placid, unruffled men with whom he presents so sharp a contrast. The further irony is that Adolphe will later become discontented with his discontent, will feel the stirring of an ambition to settle down to a regular occupation − a post worthy of his talents − and that this will eventually lead to Ellénore's illness and death. Her attractive restlessness is that of a woman no longer in her youth who is desperately looking for conventional respectability; *his* stems from the clamorous dissatisfaction of a young man of great intelligence for whom nonetheless it will be natural sooner or later to seek some accommodation with society. Age, sex, beliefs and position in society combine to produce for Adolphe and Ellénore a first impression that there is a deep kinship between them: once they are together, the reality of the different demands such forces make on them in the particular world they inhabit becomes a source of conflict and misery, and ultimately dooms their relationship.

Not only is the final note of the 'portrait' of Ellénore − the paradox/oxymoron of the *bel orage*, the 'magnificent storm' − sustained through the novel (in Chapter IV the conversation between the couple takes 'a stormy turn', and by Chapter VIII their life has become 'a perpetual storm'): one of the most remarkable features arising from the character description is that elements of it are repeated in a significantly modified form at the end of Chapter VIII. This occurs in a passage that was excluded by Constant from the first two editions of *Adolphe* but included in the third edition of 1824. The section concerns Ellénore's attempts to excite Adolphe's jealousy and may have been suppressed as being in poor taste since the reading public might have seen in it an allusion to Mme de Staël's well-known promiscuity:

Elle avait l'esprit juste, mais peu étendu; la justesse de son esprit était dénaturée par l'emportement de son caractère, et son peu d'étendue l'empêchait d'apercevoir la ligne la plus habile, et de saisir des nuances délicates. Pour la première fois elle avait un but; et comme elle se précipitait vers ce but, elle le manquait. Que de dégoûts elle dévora sans me les communiquer! que de fois je rougis pour elle sans avoir la force de le lui dire! Tel est parmi les hommes le pouvoir de la réserve et de la mesure, que je l'avais vue plus respectée par les amis du comte de P*** comme sa maîtresse, qu'elle ne l'était par ses voisins comme héritière d'une grande fortune, au milieu de ses vassaux. Tour à tour haute et suppliante, tantôt prévenante, tantôt susceptible, il y avait dans ses actions et dans ses paroles je ne sais quelle fougue destructive de la considération, qui ne se compose que du calme.   (Ch. VIII, pp. 182–3)

(She was of sound but limited intelligence: the soundness of her intellect was marred by the impetuousness of her character, and its limitations prevented her from seeing the shrewdest course of action to pursue and from perceiving subtle nuances. For the first time she had a goal, but by rushing towards it she missed it. How many humiliations she endured without telling me! How many times I blushed for her without finding the strength to tell her so! Such is the power of reserve and moderation in men that I have seen her treated with more respect by the friends of the Count when she was his mistress than she was by her neighbours as the heiress to a great fortune and surrounded by her vassals. By turn haughty and humble, sometimes considerate, sometimes hypersensitive, she displayed in her words and actions a feverish impulsiveness which cost her the respect of others − that respect which only calm can inspire.)

The passage knowingly recalls the Ellénore seen by the impartial observer while she was still living with the Comte de P*** (*esprit*, *juste*, *calme*, *fougue*), but it does so in order to emphasise how her situation has now tragically worsened. It is unmistakably the direct utterance of the narrator himself, the older Adolphe who has known her, who has experienced her limited perception, her ordinary mind, and who qualifies his words of praise (*mais . . .*), but who pities in restrospect the fact that her plan to be respected by the noble families of the region around Warsaw misfires. The very repetitiousness of

the passage when put side by side with the earlier portrait
where such care was evident in achieving variety – a faint
echo of its style being reached perhaps only in the last
sentence – this repetitiousness seems to reflect at once the
decline of Ellénore, now making a desperate and (as it turns
out) final attempt to salvage her reputation, and the narrator's own increasing loss of composure. He becomes more
exclamatory as the climax of his story approaches, and the
passage is followed by his comment: 'In listing Ellénore's failings thus it is myself I am accusing and condemning. One
word from me would have calmed her: why could I not say
it?' No longer is the observer watching the *bel orage* with
detached interest and curiosity; the storm has wrought its
devastation on the viewer who, as he remembers, now realises
in turn his responsibility for bringing to Ellénore not the calm
she needed but only destructive torment.

Chapter 7

A choice of evils

Ellénore's experience before she meets Adolphe, and *a fortiori* afterwards, is in direct contradiction to the 'parody of a well-known saying' of Adolphe's father, 'Cela leur fait si peu de mal, et à nous tant de plaisir!', 'It [i.e. a casual affair] does them so little harm and gives us so much pleasure' (Ch. I, p. 118). The novel as a whole is a darkly ironic commentary on that particular general maxim, one which is obviously untrue in the case of a woman like Ellénore, but also of a man like Adolphe, whose pleasure from the affair is short-lived. (Yet at a deeper level — and by a double irony very characteristic of Constant — would it not be true to say that Ellénore despite everything considers the world well lost for Adolphe, and that he comes to feel far more for her than he is fully aware of at the time?) The first underlying irony is that Adolphe, a specialist in *la plaisanterie*, nonetheless takes his father's quip seriously, and it brings him to despair and loneliness; the second irony is that since humour is so ingrained in him, it is natural for Adolphe to warm to anything that subverts the 'banal formulae' of society: yet what could be more unthinking than such humour as a rule of conduct, more pernicious than mere banality? Adolphe's spirit of contradiction and distrust of 'general axioms which allow for no exceptions or nuances' (Ch. I, p. 114) lead him into a different and more deadly trap. Thus, drawn on by an element of vanity to emulate a friend's success with a woman, but also feeling that need for emotional stimulus and satisfaction which I examined in an earlier chapter, he takes the fateful step of seducing Ellénore.

It would be easy to view *Adolphe* as being — as, arguably, the autobiographical *Cahier rouge* is — a carefully assembled indictment of the Father, taking as its starting-point Benjamin

Constant's own experience with Juste de Constant. Too easy, perhaps: the tragedy in the novel is undeniably in part the result of heredity and upbringing, and, later, the consequence of pressure from Adolphe's father applied with zeal and cunning by the Baron de T***. (Curiously Adolphe's father is absent from the story at the end, and his sympathy would in any case be unwelcome: we never see him regretful and penitent as we do William's father at the end of Mme de Charrière's *Caliste*.) But Adolphe makes sufficient mistakes for which he alone must be held responsible to render such a simple apportioning of blame out of the question: he knows he is right in his own judgement of Ellénore when she is misrepresented to him by the Baron (Ch. VII, pp. 170–2); he is fully aware of the proprieties and hypocrisies of polite society, and is loyal and protective towards Ellénore for much of the time, feeling responsible for her well-being despite her tyrannical possessiveness and wearying fretfulness – both of course are entirely understandable, given her situation and her feelings for him. Yet he is younger than she is, he is also an intellectual with legitimate ambitions whose talents are going to waste and who feels, as the narrator recalls, that 'it was time I devoted myself to a career, began a more active life, acquired some claim to men's esteem, and made a more noble use of my faculties' (Ch. VI, p. 162) – incidentally a verbal echo of William in *Caliste*, who in a very similar situation longs 'to make a more noble and practical use of [his] faculties than hitherto' (*O.C.*, VIII, p. 207). Adolphe wants to escape from a relationship that has lost all excitement for him, and to be reintegrated into the community.

If one looks for tragic flaws, there are obviously several: Adolphe's highly developed intellect, his capacity for 'thinking too precisely on the event' makes him ill at ease among the more commonplace minds of society, and he appears to them offensively unsure about their certainties; his unremitting analysis of his feelings for Ellénore leads him, as numerous critics have observed, to underestimate their deep-rootedness and their importance to him. Vanity is among his reasons for entering the relationship with Ellénore: well-judged flattery by the Baron de T*** prompts Adolphe to think once again about extricating himself from it. His age and inexperience — and the principal function of the older narrator is surely to emphasise this element in the drama — render Adolphe blind to the incalculable consequences of seducing a woman like Ellénore and the no less incalculable cost to both of them of abandoning her. If he had looked more closely at Ellénore before acting, he would have seen that the apparent similarities between two emotionally un-fulfilled individuals who feel themselves to be on the margins of society hide very different outlooks and aspirations, poten-tially antagonistic ones. As Constant says in the 'Preface to the Second Edition' of *Adolphe*, once these two personalities come together, they are set on a disaster course: the only solu-tion is not to become involved in such a relationship, for 'once one goes along that path, all that is left is a choice of evils' (p. 103). In the same paragraph Constant explains that he deliberately created a 'position . . . sans ressource', an in-soluble situation for both of the central characters. Every word of the novel is weighed and tested, every small detail in the drama is there to exclude the possibility of trite solutions.

It would be misguided to look for villains in *Adolphe*. The most obvious candidate, the Baron de T***, the old diplomat representing the Elector of *** in Warsaw, acts in what he sees as the best interests of the son of a friend and fellow government minister, but is blinkered by his age and experience (a curiously symmetrical counterpoint to Adolphe). For the Baron the solution to Adolphe's problem is straightforward, a mere question of will: he is unaware of how little application his views may have to the precise individuals and circumstances he is dealing with. Human limitation is likewise to blame for the unhappy history of Adolphe's relationship with his father, the latter being hampered by an apparently congenital inability to have an easy and close rapport with his son. Ellénore clings destruc-tively to the man she loves more than all else — more, it would seem, than her children or their father, the Comte de P***; without Adolphe she would be a complete social outcast. Adolphe, in addition to the other qualities we have seen in him, is by his own admission a weak man: it is this 'weakness' — the term immediately becomes problematic when set in context — which makes him stay with Ellénore when others would have left her; it is likewise this weakness, allied to his vanity, that allows him to be driven by the Baron into a corner from which he cannot escape.

Chapter 8

Adolphe and its readers

Constant's *Adolphe* is a landmark in many ways, not least because it marks an unmistakable break with a particular tradition of the French novel, a tradition which had been popular throughout the eighteenth century, the *roman libertin* or novel of seduction. In its first pages it creates something like the situation of a story by Crébillon *fils* — and then gives it a quite unheard-of twist. At its publication *Adolphe* was a *nouveau roman*, a new novel in the most useful sense of the phrase: it was a revitalisation of the genre and at the same time a renewal of accuracy and rigour in the presentation of the inner life of characters and of the pressures under which they must exist. As Paul Delbouille has shown, it met the fate often reserved for works of great originality in the form of a largely uncomprehending or hostile reading public, and many decades were to pass before it acquired the status of a classic which it now holds. Some of those closest to Constant — Mme de Staël's daughter Albertine and Constant's cousin Rosalie, for example — appreciated the subtlety of his thought and craftsmanship, but among reviewers and writers, with rare exceptions, *Adolphe*'s qualities went unrecognised. Lady Caroline Lamb, who tried to persuade the London publisher John Murray to take the novel, told him 'it is one of the cleverest things yet written but it will only make one vol.' (Nicolson, p. 244). Byron, however, who was persuaded to read the book by Mme de Staël in the summer it appeared, wrote to Samuel Rogers that it was a work 'which leaves an unpleasant impression, but very consistent with the consequences of not being in love, which is, perhaps, as disagreeable as anything, except being so' (Nicolson, p. 176).

Stendhal's review suggests that he may have allowed his feelings about the author's political and religious views to colour his reaction to the book, but in any case his temperament and the characters of his novels were a world away from the quiet anguish of *Adolphe*. Stendhal wrote in 1824 on the appearance of the third edition that Constant's book was 'a romance which has more of singularity than excellence in it . . . This novel may be called a *Marivaudage tragique*, in which all the difficulty is, not in making, as in *Marivaux'* romances a declaration of love, but a declaration of hatred. This once done, the story is at an end.' More damaging to Constant's reputation as a novelist was the opinion of one of the greatest of French nineteenth-century critics, Sainte-Beuve, who nurtured a fierce but oddly intermittent antipathy for him. In 1844 he wrote that *Adolphe* was a 'depressing book, faded and greyish in hue', while in a private note he dismissed it as 'a silly, unintelligible and absurd . . . little book, apart from one or two fine pages'. By the 1860s his evaluation was more generous, recognising it to be a 'masterpiece' but not the equal of Chateaubriand's *René*, by the side of which it seemed to him dull (*Genèse*, p. 462).

Meanwhile *Adolphe* was steadily attracting admirers further afield. In Russia Pushkin not only drew on the central figure as a model for his Eugene Onegin: it is clear from the dedication to Pushkin of Vyazemsky's translation of the novel that they had often discussed *Adolphe* together and greatly admired it. It is difficult not to be struck by the number of parallels between Tolstoy's *Anna Karenina*, begun in 1873, and Constant's novel. One's suspicion that Tolstoy had *Adolphe* very much in mind when he wrote his great novel is confirmed by the fact that the dissolute Oblonsky quotes word for word the dictum of Adolphe's father 'it does them so little harm . . .' (Part II, 14), and indeed at the root of the moral conflict which Tolstoy explores are the unequal standards applied to men and women in the matter of sexual morality by a hypocritical society. Vronsky, like Adolphe, proves not to be the complete accomplished libertine he once believed himself to be: he settles down to living with his mistress Anna, is faithful and even submissive to her. Like Adolphe's, his ambition resurfaces as he becomes increasingly bored with the relationship. Though patient in the face of Anna's growing demands, he insists on his right to some measure of freedom, and the dénouement is brought about by her wrongly concluding from a gesture of irritation on Vronsky's part that he is finishing with her. Anna's anticipation of Vronsky's remorse after her death is perhaps comparable with the tone of Ellénore's final letter to Adolphe.

It is well known that George Eliot used the sentence about 'the suffering one causes' from the 'Publisher's Reply' in *Adolphe* as epigraph to Chapter 50 of *Felix Holt, the Radical*. But perhaps as significant is her biographer Oscar Browning's attribution of the first impulse to write the *Scenes of Clerical Life* to the influence of Constant's novel. Pointing out that 'novel-writing did not come naturally to her', since she was 'from the first a student [i.e. scholar]', and that 'she moved timidly and with caution in the domain of imagination', he records:

The first stories were reproductions of her own experience; places and persons were so described as to be easily recognised, names were scarcely altered. Yet she had prepared herself for the analysis of character by careful study. I have seen a copy of Benjamin Constant's 'Adolphe', a novel of the minutest self-inspection, interlined and marked by her in every page, and thumbed so as almost to fall to pieces. From such elements were those tales produced which shook so rapidly the heart of England.

(*Life of George Eliot*, London, 1890, p. 147)

Constant's aphoristic manner would have had an immediate appeal to her, and might indeed have helped her in the development of her own characteristic style.

Despite the interest of Balzac, who was inspired by a (somewhat misleading) preface to *Adolphe* by Gustave Planche to draw on Constant's novel in his *La Muse du département* (1843), it was not until the end of the nineteenth century that *Adolphe*'s standing with the French reading public began to recover through the work of a new generation of critics unawed by Sainte-Beuve's pronouncements. Appreciative essays by Anatole France, Emile Faguet and Paul

Bourget in the 1880s recognised in *Adolphe* an outstanding example of the French novel of psychological analysis. By the 1930s, thanks in part to the scholarly writings of Gustave Rudler dating from the early years of the twentieth century, and to an increasing number of reprints of the novel, *Adolphe*'s position was secure. In the English-speaking world George Saintsbury's *History of the French Novel* (1917) did much to confirm the revised estimate of Constant's work, though his insistence on it as illustrating 'the Nemesis of Sensibility' through the fate of Adolphe would not nowadays find universal acceptance (pp. 442–9). Since the Second World War and particularly since the 1960s, *Adolphe* has been the object of unprecedented critical activity, showing itself capable of protean transformations with each new shift in taste and intellectual fashion, from John Middleton Murry's view of the novel as a prophecy of an undogmatic but revealed Christianity (*The Conquest of Death*, London, 1951) to Han Verhoeff's psychoanalytical hypothesis that Adolphe's treatment of Ellénore reflects conflicting compulsions in Constant resulting from his early loss of his mother (*'Adolphe' et Constant: une étude psychocritique*, Paris, 1976) and Eve Gonin's rewriting of the novel from the woman protagonist's viewpoint (*Le point de vue d'Ellénore: une réécriture d''Adolphe'*, Paris, 1981).

Adolphe, this story of the end of a love afffair set in a vanished society and told in the spare vocabulary of neo-classical French, presents us with the paradox of its perennial modernity. The critic and psychoanalyst Roland Jaccard has attempted to sum up the quality of its appeal for the twentieth-century reader: 'The absence in the novel of lasting impressions, the dissolving of energies, the derisive laugh in the face of the absolute, the fragmenting of experiences, these are the very mark of modernity: Adolphe was not of his time but of ours' (*Le Monde des livres*, 9 March 1984). Few novels give at one and the same time the feeling of being set at a precise location and datable period and yet of being situated somewhere outside time in some Sartrean *huis clos*. Its themes are of permanent and fundamental human importance:

isolation and loneliness; the need for love, the need to feel valued by society, and the need to be free — needs which can become intractably and fatally at odds. What we owe to others — to society, family, or the person with whom we have assumed a relationship — and what we owe to ourselves are obligations the balancing of which continue to cause the deepest anguish and perplexity. Yet *Adolphe* is also a novel whose fascination has always been the complex way in which it relates both to a life and to a corpus of work of which at least one important part, *Cécile*, was published for the first time only in 1951. The most rewarding writing on *Adolphe* has tended to avoid the sterile antagonism of the 'intrinsic' or formal close reading of the text *versus* the 'extrinsic' — historically or biographically inclined — reading. From many examples I would single out Georges Poulet's *Benjamin Constant par lui-même* (1968) and Alison Fairlie's series of articles now gathered together in *Imagination and Language* (1981), where the combination of scholarship and critical acumen has led to fresh insights.

Various narratological and structuralist investigations (Tzvetan Todorov, Michel Charles), Freudian and feminist explorations (Han Verhoeff, Eve Gonin) of the text have now been essayed. Future research might usefully engage with *Adolphe*'s connections not only with its author's life (where there are still many gaps in our knowledge, especially in the early years) and the European political and intellectual climate in which it developed, but also its intertextual links with other books and other authors: a closer consideration of the influence of Mme de Charrière and her *Caliste* would be a case in point. Asking the traditional question 'Is *Adolphe* a Romantic novel?' might now produce some interesting answers, especially in the light of Paul de Man's *The Rhetoric of Romanticism* (1984). In form and language *Adolphe* does not appear to be so, despite the occasional stylistic oddity. Yet the novel explores many conflicting dualities: between freedom and obligation, egoism and unselfishness, resentment and guilt; between alienation and the desire to be reintegrated into the social order; between certainty and uncertainty; between regretful nostalgia and anxious expectancy. Each of these motifs is liable to come into paradoxical and brief alignment with its opposite as the plot slowly and kaleidoscopically revolves before us, and as Adolphe's unsuccessful search continues in a prolonged but threatened present for some middle term that might resolve these tensions. In the last analysis such a pattern of inescapably opposed attitudes is profoundly Romantic. For as long as we, too, at the end of the twentieth century and in a very different but no less demanding society, feel the same contradictory pull, we shall remain Adolphe's contemporaries.

Guide to further reading

Editions and translations

The best edition of the French text of *Adolphe* is that by Paul Delbouille (Paris: Belles Lettres, 1977), which has a detailed introduction and notes, and which gives manuscript variants. The text of the Classiques Garnier edition by Jacques-Henry Bornecque (Paris, 1968) is less reliable, but there is a valuable introduction, contextual material and notes. Among the cheaper French editions the Garnier-Flammarion has a perceptive introduction by Antoine Adam, linking the novel with the tradition of French *moralistes* and maxim-writers which goes back to the seventeenth century. Probably the best English translation is still that of Constant's friend Alexander Walker, prepared under Constant's supervision in London, published in 1816 and deserving of a modern reprint. Among more easily available twentieth-century translations are those of Carl Wildman (with an introduction by Harold Nicolson, London, 1948, reprinted 1959), John Middleton Murry (in *The Conquest of Death*, London, 1951) and L. W. Tancock (Harmondsworth: Penguin Classics, 1964, most recently reprinted in 1985). An edition of Constant's complete works in some sixty volumes is currently being planned by an international team of scholars. Meanwhile the *Œuvres* volume edited by Alfred Roulin (Paris: Gallimard, 'Bibliothèque de la Pléiade', 1957) offers, in addition to *Adolphe*, *Cécile*, the *Cahier rouge* and the Journals, a useful annotated selection of Constant's more important political and religious writings.

Books and articles about *Adolphe* and Constant

There is now a very considerable body of writing on *Adolphe*. As a starting-point for critical reflection the following works in English can be recommended:

106

Martin Turnell, *The Novel in France*, London: Hamish Hamilton, 1950. Stimulating chapter on Constant and *Adolphe*.

I. W. Alexander, *Adolphe*, London: Edward Arnold, 'Studies in French literature', no. 24, 1973. Stresses the importance of Adolphe's relationship with Ellénore as giving meaning and purpose to his life, as a way of bringing him, in Alexander's phenomenological terminology, into relationship with 'Being'.

Alison Fairlie, *Imagination and Language. Collected Essays on Constant, Baudelaire, Nerval and Flaubert*, ed. Malcolm Bowie, Cambridge University Press, 1981. The articles on *Adolphe* which make up the first 125 pages of the book are by far the most perceptive studies of style, structure and characterisation in Constant's novel to have been written in any language, and repay close study.

Timothy Unwin, author of an important article, 'The narrator and his evolution in Constant's *Adolphe*' (*Swiss-French Studies*, III/2, 1982), is preparing a monograph on *Adolphe*, no. 58 in the Grant and Cutler series, 'Critical Guides to French Texts' (London).

In French two books in particular have made outstanding contributions to the understanding of Constant's mind and art:

Georges Poulet, *Benjamin Constant par lui-même*, Paris: Du Seuil, 'Les écrivains de toujours' series no. 78, 1968. In a brilliant essay on the experience of time in Constant's life as reflected in his varied writings, Poulet devotes some highly perceptive pages to *Adolphe*. He stresses the difficult equilibrium Adolphe achieves between his immediate fear of causing Ellénore suffering and his long-term wish to regain his independence, an equilibrium destroyed by the fatal intervention of an uninvolved third party who favours brutally clear-cut solutions (pp. 94–6).

Paul Delbouille, *Genèse, structure et destin d' 'Adolphe'*, Paris: Belles Lettres, 1971. An exhaustive study of the composition of the novel, its structure and style, and the history of its critical reception.

A number of distinguished Continental critics have written in recent years on the use of speech in *Adolphe* and on its structure, including Tzvetan Todorov ('La parole selon Constant' in *Poétique de la prose*, Paris, 1971) and Michel Charles (*'Adolphe* ou l'inconstance', in *Rhétorique de la lecture*, Paris, 1977). The journal *Annales Benjamin Constant*, edited since 1980 at the Institut Benjamin Constant, Lausanne by Etienne Hofmann, has published some notable critical essays, for example Markus Winkler's 'Benjamin Constant et la métaphore de la poussière' (no. 4, 1984) and Jean-Luc Seylaz's 'Le portrait d'Ellénore et le jeu des pronoms' (no. 5, 1985), and gives year by year a comprehensive list of all publications on Constant.

Meanwhile scholars and historians continue to produce significant re-interpretations of Constant's career and writings and thereby to shed new light on *Adolphe*, most recently:

Markus Winkler, *'Décadence actuelle': Benjamin Constants Kritik der französischen Aufklärung*, Frankfurt: Lang, 1984. A penetrating study of Constant's continuing defence of certain Enlightenment ideals under Napoleon's dictatorship, and of his simultaneous rejection of the Enlightenment's negative and inhuman side which in his eyes had brought France to a reign of tyranny.

Stephen Holmes, *Benjamin Constant and the Making of Modern Liberalism*, New Haven: Yale University Press, 1984. Holmes places *Adolphe* in the context of Constant's wider political concern with the fate of the individual in modern society.

Norman King, 'Romantisme et opposition', *Romantisme*, no. 51, 1986. By examining the use of the terms 'calcul' and 'nature' in the writings of the Coppet Group, King brings out the Group's opposition to Napoleon and to his exalting of the principle of self-interest.

Biographies and general studies

There are several good general studies of Constant's life and work in English:

Harold Nicolson, *Benjamin Constant*, London: Constable,

1949. A well-written, intelligent and eminently readable biography, albeit occasionally inaccurate.

W. W. Holdheim, *Benjamin Constant*, London: Bowes and Bowes, 1961. A useful study of Constant's intellectual development with some helpful pages on *Adolphe*.

John Cruickshank, *Benjamin Constant*, New York: Twayne World Authors, 1974. A clear account stressing the interrelatedness of Constant's political, religious and aesthetic concerns.

Finally, Michel Crouzet's *Nature et société chez Stendhal: la révolte romantique* (Villeneuve d'Ascq: Presses universitaires de Lille, 1985) uncovers in passing a number of rich and suggestive parallels between Constant and his great near-contemporary Stendhal, both in the area of their common Rousseauistic inheritance and in that of the many-sided problem of 'Romantic revolt', parallels highly pertinent to some of the issues I have raised here.